*gardening easy*

# Trees

# gardening easy

# Trees

edited by Geoff Bryant

RANDOM HOUSE
NEW ZEALAND

A RANDOM HOUSE BOOK
published by
Random House New Zealand
18 Poland Road, Glenfield, Auckland, New Zealand

www.randomhouse.co.nz

First published 2005

Photos copyright Random House Australia 2005, from the Random House Photo Library except for the following © Geoff Bryant, www.cfgphoto.com: p40 (left), p58 (left)

Text copyright Random House 2005

All rights reserved. No part of this publication may be reproduced, stored in a retrieval system, or transmitted in any form or by any means, electronic, mechanical, photocopying, recording or otherwise, without the prior written permission of the publisher.

National Library of New Zealand
Cataloguing-in-Publication data
Available on request

ISBN 1 86941 647 3

Design: Trevor Newman
Production: BookNZ (www.booknz.co.nz)
Printed by Wai Man Book Binding China Ltd.

Cover photographs:
Front cover – *Magnolia* × *soulangeana* variety
Back cover (top) *Gingko biloba*; (base) *Aesculus* × *carnea*

# Contents

Introduction 7

Species 22

Index 95

# Introduction

The influence of trees is felt in our lives every day, most especially in the air we breathe, but also in the many products that are still made from wood or timber by-products and in the processes that are fuelled by wood. Perhaps more important, though, is what trees do for our mental well-being and our appreciation of nature. Trees are undeniably beautiful and it takes a very hard heart indeed not to feel more at ease simply by being among them. And in all but the smallest or most stylized gardens, trees are a crucial part of the design, providing height, shade, wind and noise buffers, a playground, homes for garden wildlife and by providing shelter that modifies the climate beneath them.

Trees are obviously the largest plants in any garden, indeed they are among the largest living things, and it is their sheer size that is the main determining factor in how we use trees and how we adapt to living with them.

In that they determine the shape of a garden and how light and shade fall upon it, trees are framework plants. Yet they often do far more than simply shape the garden because their branches and foliage form a canopy that helps to fill in the framework that they have created. In this way a garden's trees set the tone for its other plants. Whether you choose deciduous, evergreen, tall and narrow, round-headed or spreading will greatly influence the nature of the garden beneath the canopy and the plants that it can successfully support.

A canopy of deciduous trees tends to create an open woodland that is ideal for rhododendrons, primulas, and other plants that thrive in dappled shade. Conifers, on the other hand, can produce a thick thatch of fallen needles that makes it difficult to cultivate anything beneath them. Broad-leafed evergreen trees have less effect on the soil but can block out so much light that under-planting choices may be very limited. And all trees use a considerable amount of water, even when not in leaf, and may stress the surrounding plants in times of drought.

The dividing line between trees and shrubs is not always clear-cut. While a tree is usually defined as a single-trunked, woody-stemmed plant over 13 ft (4 m) tall, many genera contain examples that blur these boundaries. Take *Magnolia × soulangeana* for example, is it a tree or a shrub? Its size suggests that it is a tree, but while it usually has just one trunk it may branch very low down, creating a shrubby effect. Ultimately the difference is not important; what matters is how the plants are used and in this you are limited only by your imagination.

## Assessing your site and soil

Creating a garden is an exciting challenge with the potential to reward you with a lifetime of enjoyment. But a new garden requires careful planning, hard work and knowledge, and before you can even think about planting you must thoroughly assess and prepare the site.

Despite their importance and influence on all other aspects of the garden, trees are often an afterthought in home gardens. They tend to be positioned to provide shade or to block undesirable views after the lawn is sown and the favorite shrubs and perennials are planted. But of course the trees should be planted first. They will be the largest plants and the longest lived and most difficult to alter once established. Yet so many people with small gardens insist on planting trees that will rapidly outgrow the site and cast the whole garden in deep shade. How often do you see trees that have outgrown the space allocated to them or that have been heavily pruned to make them fit? Don't attempt to grow a tree unless you know that you can cope with its size and that you have considered the full impact it may have on your garden.

# 8
## TREES

*Cornus nuttalii*

Before choosing any trees you need to consider the nature of your site and what the soil can best support. Considerations such as view and exposure to the prevailing winds can be quickly assessed and are usually reflected in the price of the land, but the drainage and type of soil need further investigation.

The natural contours of the site have the greatest influence on house and garden design. Severely sloping land can be difficult to work with and may complicate garden maintenance; it also demands a higher level of fitness from the gardener. However, if the slopes can be modified, either by excavation or terracing, you will find that variations in level are one of the best ways of adding interest to a garden. Where the levels can't be altered, planting trees or large shrubs is an excellent way to stabilise the land and minimize any run-off problems.

The site orientation determines how much sun various parts of the garden receive, which will affect the range of plants you can grow and may also determine how wet the soil is in winter, how quickly it warms up in spring and dries out in summer. However, this can be difficult to assess with bare land unless you know what the design of the house will be like and how it will be located. Sites that run north–south will experience greater variations in sun and shade between the front and back of the garden than those that run east–west. But until you have a clear idea of the house design it is difficult to determine exactly where light and shade will fall. The design of the surrounding houses will also have some influence and the passage of the sun through the seasons will affect various aspects of the site. Areas that are open to the high summer sun may be completely shaded in winter. Also, consider the changing angle of the sun through the seasons. Areas that receive late or early summer sun may see none in winter.

### Drainage

Drainage serves three main purposes: it directs run-off water away from the house; eliminates poorly drained garden areas; and lessens the risk of any earth movement in sloping parts of the garden. Good drainage is vital for ensuring that your house is pleasant to live in and that your garden thrives. Poor drainage can lead to rotting and mildew in the house and is tolerated by very few plants.

The top 24 in (60 cm) or so of soil can easily be altered but the subsoil is largely permanent and

*Cupressus macrocarpa*

*Albizia julibrissin*

unalterable, and it has a significant bearing on drainage. A very heavy subsoil, often known as a claypan or hard-pan, can cause otherwise vigorous young trees to struggle when their roots hit the clay. Conversely, peaty soils, which can be marvelous to work with, are often saturated with water at lower levels, leading to root rots and shallow-rooted, unstable trees.

To assess the drainage, dig several holes at least 20 in (50 cm) deep in various parts of the garden. Fill the holes with water and see how quickly they drain. If they are still holding water after three hours you will need to consider additional drainage or deep cultivation to break up the clay layer. If the holes start to fill with water naturally, it indicates that the ground-water table is high. While quite normal in winter or after heavy rain, this can otherwise indicate serious drainage problems.

Trees pump up a huge amount of water from the soil and those that can tolerate very wet soil, such as swamp cypress (*Taxodium distichum*) and tupelo (*Nyssa sylvatica*), can be used to drain wet patches.

Surface drainage, such as edging gravel or small edging gutters, will remove much of the run-off from drives and pathways, but sub-surface water is a greater problem. The only way to deal with it is to remove it by underground drains.

If you do not have access to main stormwater drains you will need to create a soak pit, which is simply a deep hole filled with coarse gravel or hardfill into which drainage water is piped and left to drain naturally. A soak pit is not practical in areas with a constantly high water table but otherwise it works well enough provided it is well below the level of the garden.

## *Installing drains*

Most gardeners are capable of designing and creating a drainage system for gradual slopes, but maintaining a constant fall over severe grades and hillsides usually requires an experienced drainlayer and possibly a surveyor.

Simple drainage systems are usually built around one or two main drains that are fed by smaller secondary drains if necessary. Generally, the main drains run with the slope of the land and the secondary drains run across and down with the slope to intersect with the main drains at an angle of about 45–60°.

Fortunately, with modern plastic drainage pipe this is no longer the tedious job that it was when clay field tiles were the only option. Perforated plastic drainage pipe comes in a variety of diameters and is easily cut, which greatly simplifies the joining of main and secondary drains.

The drains must have a gentle but constant fall of at least 4–6 in (10–15 cm) per 100 ft (30 m) of pipe and seldom need to be more than 24 in (60 cm) deep. Often, an inexperienced drainlayer will overestimate the fall and depth required, only to find the ditch getting deeper and deeper at an alarming rate. The best way around this is to measure the length of the drain and establish depths for each end. That sets the depth for each point along the ditch and enables you to check the depth as you progress with the digging.

# 10

## TREES

*Magnolia × soulangeana*

Once the ditch is dug, either by hand or mechanically, and you are satisfied with its flow it should be lined to about 6 in (15 cm) with coarse gravel. The pipe is laid on the gravel bed and is then covered with a further 6–12 in (15–30 cm) of gravel. The object of the gravel is to prevent the pipe quickly becoming clogged with silt. This will happen anyway, with time, but the gravel will considerably delay the silting period. If the main drainpipe runs to a stormwater drain, and both ends can be left open, blasting water through the pipe with a hose every few months will remove any silting.

## Preparation

Good soil is the most basic ingredient of a good garden. The ideal garden soil is well drained yet moisture retentive, rich in humus, well aerated, teeming with beneficial micro-organisms and the all-important earthworms. Few new gardens have soil anything like this and you can expect to have to put in a considerable amount of work to bring the soil up to standard.

Garden soil is composed of two parts: the topsoil and the subsoil. The topsoil is the layer of well-aerated, well-drained soil that will support plant growth. Its depth depends on the structure of the soil. A loose-textured, humus-filled topsoil will be deeper than a hard clay-based topsoil because it is better aerated. The subsoil starts at the limit of soil aeration. This anaerobic subsoil is often a different color from the topsoil and sometimes smells unpleasant. It cannot support much plant life and is generally poorly drained.

All soils benefit from incorporating plenty of high-humus compost. For trees, with their deep root systems, it is often worth hiring a large rotary hoe to ensure the compost is deeply incorporated.

If your soil is well drained and contains plenty of humus you need to do little more before planting. A light dressing of a general fertilizer will help to give the trees a start, but fertilizer is often best used after the trees have started to grow and should be applied around the drip-line, away from the trunk, in order to encourage the roots to spread as they seek moisture and nutrients.

**Opposite:** Japanese gardens

# 12
TREES

Rhododendron macabeanum

Cornus florida

## Choosing your trees

### Practical considerations

Small shrubs and perennials can be changed with ease but trees are generally permanent. So for all their undeniable beauty and utility, the first practical consideration when choosing trees is to think ahead, and not just 5 years, but 10, 20, 30 or more.

Before you visit a nursery make a careful assessment of your requirements. Decide not only on the style and size of trees you want, but where they must be placed in relation to the light and wind directions. Also, you need to have in mind what is intended to grow beneath the trees. And don't forget to consider the effect that your trees will have on your neighbors. Very few things are more likely to cause disputes than ill-placed trees.

Other than the fact that any plant you choose must be able to survive in your climate and soil, basic considerations include the following:

- Wide-spreading trees cast more shade than narrow, upright trees, which are better suited to use as windbreaks or privacy screens.
- Deciduous trees are just as effective at providing summer shade, but they let in light in winter, while evergreens provide a better year-round windbreak.
- Deciduous trees and pines usually lead to the most work removing fallen leaves and needles, though ultimately the compost they provide may be well worth the effort.
- Spring flowers may be beautiful but they can lead to masses of fruit that causes a mess when it falls.

Where you intend to plant plays a vital part in tree selection. When siting trees bear in mind the layout of household drains and sewers. Removing tree roots from a blocked sewer is not one of life's most pleasant jobs, and it's not just a matter of cleaning out the plumbing; it usually also means removing the tree. You can save a lot of work and heartache by keeping trees away from pipework, thereby minimizing the risk.

The aspect and the angle of the sun, which varies with the season, determine how much shade a tree will cast. Any large tree will provide a considerable amount of shade throughout the year, but when the sun is at its lowest in winter, a wide-spreading tree can shade an entire city garden. Dense, heavily foliaged trees provide the best privacy but have little else in their favor; they cast too much shade, are less effective as windbreaks than more permeable trees and it's very difficult to grow other plants under them.

*Melaleuca quinquenervia*

*Gleditsia tricanthos* 'Stevens'

## Ornamental considerations

### Evergreen or deciduous?
Given the choice, most gardeners will opt for evergreens over deciduous trees. However, deciduous trees have plenty to offer, not just in terms of their superiority as shade and compost providers, but as ornamental plants too. Think of deciduous trees and the first thing that comes to mind is autumn foliage, those vivid tones of yellow, orange and red, but the bright green of the new spring growth should not be underestimated. There is also a wide range of summer foliage color among the deciduous trees, the bright yellow of *Robinia* 'Frisia', the deep blackish-red of the copper beeches (*Fagus*) and the silvery grey of the weeping silver pear (*Pyrus salicifolia*), not to mention the stunning floral display of *Prunus*.

### Foliage type
Conifers are generally thought of as being evergreen trees with needle-like foliage, but a few such as the larch (*Larix*) are deciduous, while others have broad leaf-like cladophylls instead of needles. Broad-leafed trees occur in a huge range of foliage types, from the tiny leaves of *Nothofagus* to the paddle-like foliage of *Rhododendron sinogrande*. The foliage has the greatest visual impact, so give careful consideration to leaf type, size and color.

### Flowers
All broad-leaved trees flower, although not all are particularly colorful. The flowering cherries (*Prunus*), dogwoods (*Cornus*) and the large magnolias are often planted for their flowers but as far as most other temperate climate trees are concerned, flowers are often a secondary consideration. Tropical and subtropical trees are different and many have spectacular flowers. Flowers are perhaps a lesser consideration with trees, behind form and foliage.

### Bark
The bark of a tree can also be very attractive. The paper bark maple (*Acer griseum*) and silver birch (*Betula pendula*) have very distinctive bark, but few trees can match the eucalypts. This large Australian family shows an enormous variation in bark texture, color and the degree to which it peels. Some species shed their bark entirely to reveal stark white trunks, others shed flakes of bark to create a multi-colored effect, and some retain their bark, which may become a deep reddish-brown. However, unlike fallen leaves, which all gardeners know make the best compost, large pieces of bark take a long time to break down and can become a fire hazard.

Dig over the soil to about 12 in (30 cm) below the depth of the new tree's root ball and to at least 12 in (30 cm) greater diameter than its current root spread. That will allow the tree to establish new roots quickly, which will help to boost its growth and to stabilize it.

Hammer in a stout metal or wooden stake, taking care not to damage the roots. Tie the tree to the stake with flexible ties that won't cut into the bark. Remember to remove the stake after a year or so, or it may eventually rub against or cut into the bark.

## Ways to use trees

### Specimen

Specimen trees are often planted in lawns but they can be sited anywhere. The important thing is that such trees should have one or more striking feature that enables them to stand alone. It can be beautiful flowers, stunning autumn foliage, stark winter bark or simply an extremely graceful habit. Whatever the feature it should be strong enough that it is not necessary to add extras in the way of flowering annuals or ornaments.

### Shade

Shade trees are usually chosen for their shape. A clean trunk with a lacy, open foliage canopy is best, providing adequate shade without creating an enclosed, dark cavern below. *Albizia julibrissin*, *Gleditsia triacanthos* and *Schinus molle* var. *areira* are good examples. Deciduous trees are generally preferred as they allow in winter sunlight.

### Avenue

Avenue trees are usually a combination of shade and specimen tree. Often they are deciduous, to allow winter light, and they frequently have a striking feature, such as flowers or colored foliage, but most important is that they will grow evenly and successfully when quite closely spaced but not so close as to form a hedge. The silver birch (*Betula pendula*) is a classic avenue tree because it is light and airy, has beautiful bark and can be stunning in autumn, though its roots may eventually lift paving.

### Shelter

Shelter trees tend to be quite densely planted and may be frequently trimmed to form a hedge. Plants such as *Cupressus macrocarpa* withstand this kind of treatment well. Naturally narrow trees, such as *Pittosporum eugenioides*, also make good shelter plants and require less trimming than spreading species.

### Woodland

Woodland trees are chosen for their ability to provide a protective canopy for the smaller plants below. They may be evergreen or deciduous, depending on the nature of the understorey planting and can be quite drab trees as they will seldom be the center of attraction. Maples, oaks and beeches are perhaps the classic woodland trees.

Opposite: *Fagus sylvatica* '(Purpurea) Tricolor'

Saw off side branches, leaving a slight stub. Be sure to undercut first.

*Paulownia tomentosa* trees frame a conservatory.

## Environmental considerations

Native trees are often undervalued, usually for no reason other than that we tend to disregard the plants that occur naturally around us. Many native trees have attractive flowers and foliage and also enhance the survival prospects for native wildlife, including birds and insects. Much of the world was tree covered for thousands of years before today's garden plants arrived and we should not underestimate the value and beauty of the native flora.

## At the nursery

Having made up your mind what you need and how to follow a sensible course of action it is all too easy to arrive at the nursery and then be overwhelmed by the choice available. You also need to take care to get the right information. Sometimes that comes from the nursery staff but more often than not it is a matter of applying a little common sense.

Nursery labels usually state plant size at 5–10 years old, which is fine for shrubs but rarely of much practical use with trees. The important point to remember is that a tree will continue to grow for as long as it lives. Sure, they may slow down with maturity but they will keep on growing, and not just higher, but wider too.

These days most nursery plants are container grown, but large specimens of deciduous trees are an exception and may have been lifted from the open ground before potting. Try to ensure that the trees you choose have settled down well after being lifted and that they are well established but have not been potted for so long as to have become root bound. A gentle prodding of the soil usually reveals how tightly packed the roots are.

Choose trees that are well shaped, with a strong trunk and even branching. When selecting trees with variegated or colored foliage avoid those that show any signs of reverting to plain green.

Lastly, if in any doubt about the suitability of a tree, leave it and come back later. Trees are simply too permanent to rush into planting. Your local parks and gardens will probably have specimens of those that interest you and seeing the mature trees will provide the answers to most questions.

## Planting and maintenance

Prior to planting, work in plenty of fine compost to improve the soil texture and increase its moisture retention and dig over the soil to about 12 in (30 cm) below the depth of the new tree's root ball and to at least 12 in (30 cm) greater diameter than its current root spread. This will allow it to establish new roots quickly, which will help to boost growth and to stabilize it.

Carefully remove the tree from its container and plant to the same depth as it was in the

*Fagus sylvatica* 'Tricolor'

container; a soil mark is usually clearly visible on the trunk. If the surface roots are showing you may plant a little deeper but take care that you don't bury the union point of grafted or budded trees. Hammer in a stout stake before finally firming the tree into place, taking care not to damage the roots. The ground around the tree will need to be trodden down somewhat to firm it, but it's better to firmly stake the tree and keep the soil loose than it is to compact down all that soil you laboriously loosened up. In very dry areas or where the tree must fend for itself it's often a good idea to make a small ridge of soil around the drip-line. This ensures that any moisture dripping from the foliage is channeled back to the roots.

Having planted the tree you may feel the need to add fertilizer, but if you apply fertilizer before the tree begins to grow it may develop a too-compact root system because there is no need for new roots to seek out soil nutrients. When you apply fertilizer put it just outside the drip-line and water it in well to encourage the roots to spread downward and outward.

Trees are at their most vulnerable during the first two years after planting. Established trees can largely look after themselves. Trimming to shape, loosening ties and restaking, fertilizing, watering and controlling pests and diseases are all necessary to ensure that your trees get the best start.

Remove any weeds that appear and use mulch to control their development. The mulch also conserves moisture, reducing the amount of watering needed. Water when the weather is dry. Don't just sprinkle—wetting the soil surface alone does more harm than good because it encourages the development of roots close to the surface, where they suffer when the soil dries out again. The aim is to encourage the roots to go deep where the soil dries out more slowly. Not often but thoroughly is the rule.

Water retention varies with the soil type: sandy soils absorb water quickly, but don't hold it well and so dry out fast; clay soils absorb it slowly but hold it for longer. Water evaporates from the soil faster on hot days—and on windy ones—than it does in cooler weather. Watering in the heat of the day is wasteful, as much of your water will evaporate; the early morning or evening is preferable. Take care in adjusting your sprinklers so they don't deliver water faster than the soil can absorb it.

Mulching with compost or well-rotted manure fertilizes the soil as well as stemming moisture loss; this can be boosted with a light dressing of something more concentrated as the regular growing season begins. Artificial fertilizer is fine, but it doesn't maintain the essential humus on which the continued health of the soil depends. For that, organic material is needed. Happily, many trees supply their own by dropping their leaves. Leaving these to rot where they fall is one of the few times in life when laziness is rewarded!

Established trees benefit from feeding, but you need to get the fertilizer down deep where the roots are. Make a number of holes about 3 ft (1 m) apart across the entire spread of the roots. These should be about 2 in (5 cm) wide and at least 20 in (50 cm) deep. Divide the allowance of fertilizer by the number of holes and pour in the calculated amount, watering it in thoroughly.

*Jacaranda mimosifolia*

## Pruning and trimming

There is a difference between pruning and trimming. Pruning is a training method, cutting a plant to make it grow in a desired direction or shape or encouraging the growth of a particular structure. Trimming is simply removing excess growth and reshaping an already existing structure.

Pruning promotes strong new growth, and helps produce a well-shaped healthy plant with a good crop of fruit or flowers. It also maintains ventilation, which reduces fungus problems, and allows light to penetrate to the center of the tree.

Unless you intend to train them to a specific shape or style of growth, the pruning of young trees is generally just a matter of removing any damaged branches and those that are likely to head off at strange angles. Most trees look better if they're allowed to develop naturally. Just aim to maintain a good branch structure with an even foliage cover.

When shaping a tree you must have an understanding of the way it develops. Severe trimming is damaging in most cases. Not only does it produce misshapen plants, it can also weaken them by removing so much foliage as to dramatically lessen their photosynthetic ability.

Heavy pruning can also produce branches that grow at acute angles. These are more easily damaged by wind or may eventually break under their own weight. Careful trimming and thinning, however, can strengthen a tree by removing weak branches and enabling it to channel its energies into stronger growth.

Consider the ultimate shape of the tree before you cut. Bearing in mind that any branch will tend to shoot from the bud immediately below a cut, it's clear that if the center is to remain open you must cut to buds facing away from the center of the plant. These are known as outward-facing buds. Sometimes you may wish to leave a few inward-facing buds to fill in the center of an otherwise loose-growing tree.

### The practice of pruning

The right time to prune depends on the type of plant and the severity of your winter climate. Hardy deciduous trees are usually best pruned in the winter. They are unlikely to be damaged by the cold and will be less likely to bleed (ooze sap) during winter. Spring-flowering trees should be pruned soon

*Robinia hispida*

after flowering rather than in winter, which would remove the flower buds. Pruning frost-tender trees is best left until spring because cutting them in winter only exposes the vulnerable cut stems to more frost damage. Spring pruning will still allow for an entire season's growth before the next winter.

There's usually no reason why you shouldn't trim and thin in summer too. Shaping during the growing season, when you can readily see the effects, is often easier than trying to envisage exactly how the growth will develop after winter pruning. But don't cut back in early spring when the sap is flowing quickly because the cuts can bleed excessively and may refuse to heal properly.

How far to cut back is a question that always leads to confusion. You can find all sorts of theories about how hard to cut back and why, but it all comes down to the initial reasons for pruning: renewing vigor, maintaining health and shaping. As mentioned earlier, too severe a trimming may actually lead to reduced vigor and a poorly shaped plant.

Ensure that your pruners (and saws or loppers too, if heavier equipment is needed) are sharp so that all the cuts are clean. Trim so that water runs away from the bud. When trimming heavy branches remember to first make an undercut on the lower side to avoid the bark tearing as the branch falls.

The exact method of cutting is open to debate. The old school of thought was to cut side-branches as flush as possible to the main stem, then seal the wound with a pruning paste or paint. Recent research suggests that it may be better to leave a stub, or crown, and use pruning paste (preferably one with antibacterial agents) only on plants that are prone to infection, such as those of the rose family. This appears to better replicate what happens when a shrub suffers natural damage, encouraging a more rapid formation of callus tissue and therefore quicker healing. The general methods for pruning are as follows:

- Completely remove any diseased, damaged or weak wood.
- Remove suckers and overly vigorous water-shoots.
- Locate the healthy main stems and branches formed during last season's growth.
- Cut back to healthy outward-facing buds.
- Assess the results and adjust as necessary.

Cuts to large branches may benefit from sealing with pruning paint or paste but as mentioned above there are doubts about its long-term merits. It may prevent immediate fungal infection but could also slow down or prevent proper healing.

Because you may have disturbed fungal spores that will find an easy entry to the plant by way of the freshly cut stems, always remove any fallen debris and spray with a fungicide after pruning.

## Transplanting trees

Moving a mature tree is rarely practical without professional help, but many young or small trees can be successfully transplanted. The best candidates for transplanting have densely fibrous root systems, like rhododendrons, while some trees, such as eucalypts, invariably collapse after transplanting, regardless of the level of care taken.

Preparation for transplanting should begin well beforehand, with pruning of the roots. This reduces the root ball to a manageable size and provokes the growth of a mass of fine new roots to nourish the tree in its new home and, incidentally, to bind the root ball together when it is lifted from the ground. Cut a circular trench about a third of the way out from the main stems to the outer branches and as deep as possible, using sharp spades and pruners if big roots are encountered. Then fill in with fine soil enriched with organic matter, watering as you fill.

At transplanting time (usually mid- to late winter) dig beneath the root ball, and sever the roots that you left earlier. Lift and transport the tree by cradling it from below. If the tree is picked up by its stems the roots could tear off, and the tender bark may be crushed.

Position the transplant at precisely the same depth as before. Orient it as before, so the same side will be in the sun. Do not loosen the soil from the roots. If the tree is a big one, the weight of the root ball may be enough to keep it steady once in place, otherwise use stakes.

If successful it will still be at least two years before the tree is fully re-established and is able to look after itself. In the meantime, water regularly, and fertilize in spring.

## Hardiness zones

For each plant listed in this book, both a minimum and maximum zone number is indicated. These zone numbers are based on world geographical zones of expected minimum winter temperatures, which may limit the survival of cultivated plants. Plants will survive average winter frosts expected in at least the warmer part of the lower numbered zone, and will grow reasonably well in up to at least the cooler part of the higher zone number.

| Zone | °F | °C | Zone | °F | °C |
|---|---|---|---|---|---|
| 0 | no plant life | | | | |
| 1 | below −50 | below −46 | 2 | −50 to −40 | −46 to −40 |
| 3 | −40 to −30 | −40 to −34 | 4 | −30 to −20 | −34 to −28 |
| 5 | −20 to −10 | −28 to −21 | 6 | −10 to 0 | −21 to −16 |
| 7 | 0 to 10 | −16 to −12 | 8 | 10 to 20 | −12 to −7 |
| 9 | 20 to 30 | −7 to −1 | 10 | 30 to 40 | −1 to 4 |
| 11 | 40 to 50 | 4 to 10 | 12 | 50 to 60 | 10 to 16 |

Abies concolor var. lowiana

Abies lasiocarpa 'Compacta'

*Firs are among the most stately of all conifers.*

# Abies
*Fir*

The true firs, sometimes known as silver firs to distinguish them from *Picea* (which have pendent, not upright, cones), comprise about 40 species of evergreen conifers. Among the most stately of all conifers, firs come from cool- to cold-climate mountain areas of the northern hemisphere. Most are from China and western North America, but a few species extend into the tropics on the high mountains of Central America and Southeast Asia. The short, stiff needles, which are distributed evenly along the twigs, usually have 2 longitudinal blue bands on their undersides.

## Cultivation

Their narrow shape and often slow growth allow many species to fit comfortably into the larger suburban garden, but they will not tolerate urban pollution and prefer a moist climate without extremes of heat. Soils must have adequate depth, drainage and moisture retention. Propagation is from seed. Grafting is used for selected clones, including named cultivars. The only pruning or shaping needed is the removal of twin leading shoots as soon as they appear.

### Abies concolor

**Colorado fir, White fir**

This species grows wild in the Rocky Mountains of western USA, where it reaches 150 ft (45 m); a taller race, ***Abies concolor* var. *lowiana*** (Pacific fir) is found closer to the coast in Oregon and northern California. The needles, which are bluish-green on both sides and blunt-tipped, exude a lemon scent when bruised. Cones range from deep dull purple to pale brown. A fine ornamental fir, it is also hardy and vigorous. Seedlings vary in the blueness of their foliage. Some of the best blue forms, propagated by grafting, are sold under the name '**Glauca**'; even more striking is the rare and slower-growing pale blue cultivar '**Candicans**'. Zones 5–9.

### Abies lasiocarpa

**Subalpine fir, Rocky Mountain fir**

This species grows up to the tree line in the Rocky Mountains, from Arizona to southern Alaska. It may be a 100 ft (30 m) tall tree or a horizontal spreading shrub. The needles are crowded and overlapping, with bluish stripes on both surfaces. Cones are fat and dark purple. To the southeast of its range the typical species is replaced by ***Abies lasiocarpa* var. *arizonica***, the corkbark fir, which has thick, corky, pale bark and blue-gray foliage. Selections of this variety valued as garden plants include '**Compacta**', silver-blue and slow growing but difficult to obtain as it is propagated by grafting, and '**Aurea**', which has yellowish foliage. Zones 4–9.

### Abies pinsapo

**Spanish fir**

A handsome column-shaped tree reaching 100 ft (30 m), often with multiple leaders and densely crowded branches, this fir adapts to a wide range of soils and climates. The very short, rigid needles are less flattened than in most firs, and have fine bluish-white stripes on both surfaces. In spring small purple pollen cones appear on the lower branch tips. The seed cones, produced near the top of the tree, are brown when ripe. Seedlings are selected for bluish foliage, collectively referred to under the cultivar name '**Glauca**'. Zones 5–9.

# Acacia
syn. *Racosperma*
*Wattle*

This large genus contains over 1200 species of trees and shrubs from warm climates. Some are deciduous

Acacia baileyana     Acacia longifolia

but most are evergreen. Over 700 are indigenous to Australia. They range from low-growing shrubs to tall trees and many have been introduced to other countries for economic and ornamental purposes. They are also common in tropical and subtropical Africa. Acacias have either bipinnate leaves or their leaves are replaced by flattened leaf stalks, known as phyllodes. The tiny flowers, ranging from deep golden-yellow to cream or white, and crowded into globular heads or cylindrical spikes, are often fragrant and produce abundant, bee-attracting pollen. Fruit is either round or flattened pods.

## Cultivation

The hard-coated seeds remain viable for up to 30 years. They should be treated by heating and soaking for germination in spring. Some need fire to germinate. In cultivation many species are fast-growing but short-lived (10–15 years). In their native regions they are often disfigured by insect or fungus attack. They do best in full sun and well-drained soil. Some will tolerate part-shade.

### Acacia baileyana

**Cootamundra wattle, Golden mimosa**

A fast-growing, small, spreading tree to 20 ft (6 m), the Cootamundra wattle has a short trunk and arching branches, feathery blue-gray leaves, and fragrant golden-yellow flower clusters in late winter. Widely used in warm-temperate gardens as a feature or shade tree, a specimen in full bloom can be a spectacular sight. Like most acacias, it tends to be short-lived and prone to borer attack when declining. The cultivar '**Purpurea**' has purplish foliage, especially on the growing tips. Zones 8–10.

### Acacia longifolia

**Sydney golden wattle**

Native to the eastern Australian coast, this shrub has a height and spread of up to 15 ft (4.5 m), a short trunk and irregularly shaped head. A semi-prostrate form, **Acacia longifolia var. sophorae**, may be found on exposed coastal dunes. It has narrow, oblong, dark green phyllodes and long fingers of fragrant, butter-yellow flowers in late winter and early spring. It is ideal for a seaside hedge, windbreak, or street planting. Zones 9–11.

### Acacia pycnantha

**Golden wattle**

A medium shrub or small tree up to about 20 ft (6 m) in height, this wattle is Australia's national floral emblem. In the wild it occurs mainly in Victoria and South Australia. It has a rounded crown with somewhat pendulous branches. Large, fragrant, golden, ball-shaped flowerheads are borne in spring. Although not long-lived, it makes a fine garden specimen. It prefers sandy soils and needs shelter from heavy frost. Established trees tolerate quite dry conditions. Zones 9–11.

## ACER

*Maple*

Maples are unrivaled for their autumn foliage coloring and variety of leaf shape and texture. They are also grown for shade and for timber. Many are compact enough for the average garden. The distinctive 2-winged fruit (samaras) are more noticeable than the flowers, which in most species are inconspicuous. Attractive bark is a feature of some maples—usually smooth and gray or greenish. Most species come from East Asia, particularly China (over 80 species), Japan (over 20) and the eastern Himalayas; 9 species are native to North America and a few to Europe. Most are deciduous but there are a few evergreen and semi-evergreen species from northern Turkey and the Caucasus.

*Acer griseum*

*Acer negundo*

## Cultivation

Most maples prefer a cool, moist climate with ample rainfall in spring and summer. A planting position sheltered from strong winds suits them best. For best autumn color, grow them in a neutral to acid soil. Propagation is generally from seed for the species, by grafting for cultivars. Cuttings are difficult to root, but layering of low branches can be successful. Seed germination can be aided by overwintering in damp litter, or by refrigeration. Some species produce few fertile seeds, so it may be necessary to sow a large quantity to obtain enough seedlings.

## Acer davidii

### Father David's maple

This Chinese maple of open habit and flat-topped outline is named after its discoverer, French missionary-naturalist Armand David. The scope of this name has now been widened to include a number of subspecies, previously regarded as distinct species; David's original form is placed under **Acer davidii subsp. *davidii***. A snakebark maple, it has bark striped silvery gray on an olive green background and leaves that are long pointed but mostly unlobed. Autumn brings shades of yellow, orange and dull scarlet. In a cool, humid climate it grows rapidly to 20–25 ft (6–8 m). **A. d. subsp. *grosseri*** (syns *Acer grosseri*, *A. hersii*) differs in its shorter broader leaves with 2 short lateral lobes. This tree has an overall green coloring in summer, the bark striped paler gray-green; autumn tones are similar to subsp. *davidii*. Both subspecies are popular and are easily grown from fresh seed, but chance hybrids with other nearby snakebarks are likely. Zones 6–9.

## Acer griseum

### Paperbark maple

Prized for its bark—chestnut brown with paler corky dots, which it sheds each year in wide curling strips—this narrow-crowned tree grows to 30 ft (9 m) with a straightish trunk. In autumn its small, dark green leaves turn deep scarlet. In moist, sheltered conditions with good soil, growth can be rapid. No longer common in the wild in its native China, in cultivation it produces mostly infertile seed. Zones 5–9.

## Acer negundo

### Box-elder maple, Box elder

The only North American maple to have compound leaves (consisting of 3 to 7 leaflets), this species can reach 50 ft (15 m) with a thick trunk and upright branching habit, but is more often seen as a smaller tree with cane-like bright green branches. It is fast growing and tolerates poor conditions but its branches break easily in high winds. In some areas it is regarded as a weed because of its free-seeding habits. Its several subspecies extend south into Mexico and Guatemala. Favorite cultivars include '**Elegans**', '**Variegatum**' and '**Aureo-marginatum**', with leaflets that are edged white or gold respectively; '**Aureo-variegatum**' has leaflets with broader, deeper yellow margins, retaining this coloring into autumn; the newer '**Flamingo**' is similar to '**Variegatum**' but with leaves that are strongly flushed with pink on the new growth. The male clone '**Violaceum**' has purplish new shoots and twigs; the male flower tassels are also pale purple. None of these cultivars reaches much more than half the size of the wild, green-leafed type. Zones 4–10.

## Acer palmatum

### Japanese maple

The Japanese maple is the most widely grown maple in gardens. It is valued for its compact size, delicate ferny foliage, and brilliant autumn coloring—from rich gold to deepest blood-red. In a garden it grows to 12–15 ft (3.5–4.5 m), branching

**Opposite:** *Acer palmatum* 'Dissectum'

*Acer platanoides*  *Acer pseudoplatanus* 'Erythrocarpum'  *Aesculus × carnea*

low, with strong sinuous branches and a dense, rounded crown. Although more tolerant of warmer climates than most maples, it needs shade and shelter or leaves may shrivel. The more than 300 cultivars range from rock-garden miniatures to vigorous small trees, with a great variety of leaf shape, size and coloration. Nearly all need to be grafted to preserve their characteristics, so they are expensive. The most popular cultivar of tree size is '**Atropurpureum**', dense and spreading, with dark purple spring foliage turning paler olive-purple in summer and deep scarlet tones in autumn; it usually comes true from seed. '**Sangokaku**' ('**Senkaki**') has coral-red branches and twigs, which are displayed bare in winter; in autumn leaves have brilliant gold tones. '**Atrolineare**' has foliage color like '**Atropurpureum**' but leaves divided almost to the base into narrow lobes. In the **Dissectum Group**, the primary leaf lobes are deeply cut into a filigree pattern; their fine, drooping twigs grow down rather than upward, so they are grafted onto a standard. Other well-known cultivars include '**Bloodgood**', '**Butterfly**', '**Chitoseyama**', '**Dissectum Atropurpureum**', '**Koreanum**', '**Linearilobum Rubrum**', '**Osakazuki**' and '**Shigitatsu Sawa**'. Zones 5–10.

### Acer platanoides

**Norway maple**

This maple ranges from north of the Arctic Circle in Scandinavia across Europe, from France to the Urals, but is not found in the Mediterranean or the UK, though cultivated there for centuries. A large, round-headed tree, it thrives in a wide range of soils and situations, but not in warm climates. Yellow flowers appear before the leaves; autumn color is gold to reddish-orange. Popular cultivars include '**Oregon Pride**', '**Cleveland**', '**Summershade**' and '**Drummondii**', which has variegated leaves. Cultivars with deep purplish foliage include '**Schwedleri**', '**Faassen's Black**' and '**Crimson King**'. '**Columnare**', with plain green leaves, has a narrow column shape. Zones 4–9.

### Acer pseudoplatanus

**Sycamore maple**

This species, which occurs naturally from Portugal to the Caspian Sea and has been long established in England and North America, seeds so profusely that it is regarded as a weed. Cultivated trees are 40–60 ft (12–18 m) tall and form a broad, dense, dark green crown. The thick, scaly bark is pale gray. Autumn color is not a feature. A useful park and street tree, it prefers a sheltered situation with deep moist soil, but tolerates more exposed sites. The cultivar '**Purpureum**' has leaves with deep plum undersides, the upper-sides also slightly purplish. '**Erythrocarpum**' has red fruit in conspicuous clusters. The spring foliage of '**Brilliantissimum**' is pale creamy yellow flushed pink, changing in summer to whitish with green veining; it is slow growing and suits smaller gardens; '**Rubicundum**' has leaves flecked deep pink. '**Variegatum**' has cream markings. Zones 4–10.

## Aesculus

*Horse-chestnut, Buckeye*

These deciduous trees and shrubs have a finger-like arrangement of leaflets and bear eye-catching spikes of cream to reddish flowers at the branch ends in spring or summer. The large, nut-like seeds, released from round capsules, resemble chestnuts but are bitter and inedible. At least half of the 20 or so species occur in North America; the remainder are scattered across temperate Asia and Europe. Renowned as majestic park and avenue trees in European cities, in the wild they grow mainly on valley floors, where there is shelter, deep soil and good moisture.

*Aesculus hippocastanum*

> Horse-chestnuts are renowned as majestic park and avenue trees in European cities.

*Ailanthus altissima*

## Cultivation

Although most are frost hardy, they perform best in cool climates where seasons are sharply demarcated and summers are warm. They are propagated from seed or, in the case of selected clones and hybrids, by bud grafting.

### Aesculus × carnea

**Red horse-chestnut**

This hybrid tree, thought to have originated by chance in Germany in the early 1800s, grows to about 30 ft (9 m) and often comes true from seed. It gets the reddish pink of its flowers (borne in late spring) from one parent, *Aesculus pavia*; the other parent is *A. hippocastanum*. It adapts to warmer and drier climates than *A. hippocastanum*. The cultivar '**Briotii**' has larger spikes of brighter pink flowers. Zones 6–9.

### Aesculus hippocastanum

**Horse-chestnut**

This tree originated in the mountain valleys of the Greece–Albania border region and is now widely planted in parks, avenues and large gardens in Europe. It can reach 100 ft (30 m), though is usually half that. Striking 'candles' of bloom are borne in spring and early summer; individual flowers have crumpled white petals with a yellow basal patch that ages to dull red. Fruit have a leathery case covered with short prickles and in autumn release large seeds, known as 'conkers' to British children. The dark green foliage turns yellow-brown in autumn. '**Baumannii**' has longer-lasting double flowers. Zones 6–9.

## AILANTHUS

*Tree of heaven, siris*

This tree genus from eastern Asia and the Pacific region includes both winter-deciduous and dry-season-deciduous species, though only the former are generally cultivated. They are vigorous growers of medium size, with long pinnate leaves and branches terminating in large flower clusters. Male and female flowers are produced on separate trees and neither is very conspicuous, but those on female trees develop in summer into masses of winged, papery fruits that are very decorative. The winter-deciduous species are frost-hardy trees that adapt well to urban areas, even coming up from self-sown seed in the cracks of paving. They tolerate hard pruning, responding with vigorous new growths.

## Cultivation

They do best in warm-temperate areas but will survive in most climates, preferring full sun or partial shade and deep, rich soil. Propagation is by means of seed in autumn and suckers or root cuttings from the female tree in winter.

### Ailanthus altissima

syn. *Ailanthus glandulosa*
**Tree of heaven**

Native to China, in some cities this tree is valued for its ability to withstand urban pollution; in other areas it is scorned as a weed. Planted on a large lawn it shows little inclination to sucker, growing to 50 ft (15 m), its dome-shaped crown scattered with bunches of pale reddish-brown fruits in summer. The deep green, pinnate leaves, up to 3 ft (1 m) long on young trees, smell unpleasant if bruised. Zones 6–10.

## ALBIZIA

For the most part *Albizia* species are quick-growing tropical trees and shrubs. They have feathery leaves and densely clustered small flowers with stamens far longer and more conspicuous than the petals. In the

*Albitzia julibrissin*

*Amelanchier lamarckii*          *Araucaria araucana*

wild, they are often rather weedy small trees and frequently short-lived, but can be shapely.

## Cultivation

Springing up quickly from seed, *Albizia* species are easy to cultivate, requiring summer warmth and moisture and a reasonably sheltered site.

### Albizia julibrissin

**Silk tree**

Ranging from Iran east to China, this deciduous tree is named for the long, silky stamens, creamy white to deep pink, the visible part of the flowerheads, borne in summer. Often less than 6 ft (1.8 m) tall, but flowering freely, in ideal conditions it becomes a flat-crowned tree, 20–25 ft (6–8 m) tall, with luxuriant feathery foliage. The compressed seed pods are quite prominent. It likes a warm-temperate climate and thrives in large containers but seldom lives beyond 30 years. Exceptionally richly colored specimens are usually given the name ***Albizia julibrissin* var. *rosea***. Zones 8–10.

## AMELANCHIER

Serviceberry, Snowy mespilus, Juneberry

These shrubs and small trees, mostly native to cool regions of North America, belong to the pome-fruit group of trees and shrubs in the rose family, which includes apples, pears and quinces as well as many 'berry' shrubs. Most *Amelanchier* species are deciduous, with simple oval leaves and clusters of white flowers, frequently with long narrow petals. The small rounded fruit ripen to purple or black and are often sweet and edible. Some species make attractive, graceful trees, valued for the display of snowy white flowers in spring and for their autumn coloring.

## Cultivation

They do best in moist, fertile soil in a grassy glade with the shelter of other trees but receiving ample sun. Propagation is normally from seed or by layering.

### Amelanchier lamarckii

The origin of this species has been the subject of speculation: in the past it has been much confused with *Amelanchier canadensis* and *A. laevis*. It makes a spreading shrub or small tree to 30 ft (9 m). The leaves are broad and deep green, with a coating of silky hairs when young. White flowers appear in spring in drooping clusters; small edible fruit ripen to black. Zones 6–9.

## ARAUCARIA

This remarkable, ancient genus of evergreen conifers is confined in the wild to South America, Australia, Norfolk Island, New Guinea and New Caledonia. Most are large trees with massive, straight trunks that continue to the apex of the tree, sharply distinct from the crowded, shorter, lateral branches. The leathery leaves are incurved and densely overlapping in some species, flatter and spreading in others. Male and female cones are borne on the same tree; the round, bristly seed cones develop right at the top of the trees.

## Cultivation

Most are too large for gardens but may be used as park and street trees. They will grow in a range of soil types but prefer a deep, moist, well-drained soil and full sun. Growth may be quite fast when conditions suit them. Propagate from seed in spring.

### Araucaria araucana

syn. *Araucaria imbricata*
**Monkey puzzle**

From South America, this tree enjoyed fad status in Britain in the 1840s. The remark that 'it would

Araucaria heterophylla　　　　Arbutus unedo　　　　Azara microphylla

puzzle a monkey to climb it' gave rise to the common name monkey puzzle. It can grow 80 ft (24 m) tall and 4 ft (1.2 m) in trunk diameter. Young trees have a dome-like shape with interwoven branches; with age, the crown retreats to high above the ground, so that old trees resemble long-stemmed parasols. The glossy, dark green leaves are rigid and fiercely prickly. Globular cones, 4–6 in (10–15 cm) long, are carried high on the crowns of mature trees. It needs a climate where the summers are cool and misty. Zones 8–9.

### Araucaria heterophylla

**syn. *Araucaria excelsa***
**Norfolk Island pine**

This Norfolk Island native is widely planted in subtropical coastal regions. It is upright with a regular branching pattern, conical form and grows fast to 100 ft (30 m) or more. It is wind tolerant, retaining a quite vertical and symmetrical habit even in the face of incessant onshore gales, and can thrive in deep sand. It needs reliable water when young, but can tolerate dry spells once established. Shade tolerant when young, it can be long lasting in pots. Zones 10–11.

## ARBUTUS

Strawberry tree, Madrone

A dozen or more species of evergreen tree belong to this genus, the majority from Mexico and the remainder found in the Mediterranean region and North America. Most are smallish trees with thick trunks and somewhat sinuous limbs; the bark often peels attractively. The thick-textured leaves are usually finely toothed and the flowers are small, white or pinkish bells in compact clusters at the branch ends. Some flowers develop into fleshy but hard, reddish-yellow globular fruit, often with wrinkled surfaces, which take almost a year to ripen. This 'strawberry' fruit is edible but hardly palatable.

### Cultivation

All *Arbutus* species prefer cool, humid climates, but tolerate dry conditions in summer; continental climates with extreme heat and cold do not suit them. They adapt equally to peaty, acid soils and limestone soil. Propagation is normally from seed, easily extracted from the fleshy fruit. Plant young: they dislike root disturbance.

### Arbutus unedo

**Arbutus, Strawberry tree**

Native to the western Mediterranean and Ireland, this bushy-crowned, small tree can attain 30 ft (9 m), though 10–15 ft (3–4.5 m) is usual in gardens. The bark is dark gray-brown, rather fibrous and scaly, and the smaller branches and twigs have a reddish hue. In autumn the white or pinkish flower clusters, along with the 1 in (25 mm) orange fruit from the previous year, contrast with the dark foliage. It is fairly frost hardy and will tolerate neglect, but dislikes shade and damp ground. **'Compacta'** is a smaller cultivar. Zones 7–10.

## AZARA

The 15 or so species of this temperate South American genus of shrubs and small trees include trees from Chilean subantarctic rainforests to drier slopes of the lower Andes. They have neat, glossy, evergreen foliage and massed, small yellow flowers. A characteristic feature is the way each branch node has one small and one larger leaf. While they are quite attractive plants, azaras develop a certain 'legginess' with age.

### Cultivation

Azaras prefer cool but mild and humid climates and grow best in sheltered sites in moist soil. In colder areas, they can be trained against walls to protect them from severe frosts. Propagate from cuttings in summer.

*ksia serrata*     *Banksia integrifolia*     *Betula papyrifera*

### Azara microphylla

This fairly erect, small tree may reach 20 ft (6 m) in the garden, more in the wild in its native Chile and western Argentina. A vigorous grower with fine foliage, in late winter it produces many clusters of tiny, fragrant flowers half-hidden under the leaf sprays. The most adaptable member of the genus, but sometimes damaged by frost in southern England, '**Variegata**' has attractive cream variegations. Zones 7–9.

## BANKSIA

Named after the renowned English botanist Sir Joseph Banks, who discovered this genus at Botany Bay in 1770, *Banksia* consists of about 75 species of shrubs and small trees found widely in Australia, especially in the southwest. Habit and foliage vary, but all species have striking, dense, fuzzy spikes or heads of tightly packed, small flowers, followed by woody fruits that protrude from among the dead flowers. The leaves are generally long and narrow, often with toothed edges, and contain much woody tissue, so they remain stiff and springy, even when dead. Banksias vary in their tolerance of garden conditions, but some are easily grown; the most decorative ones are now grown in plantations for the cut-flower market. The flowers of all species are rich in nectar and attract birds.

### Cultivation

Most species prefer well-drained, sandy soil with low levels of major nutrients, especially phosphates. They do best in full sun, and some are moderately frost hardy. Regular, light tip pruning maintains shape and foliage density. Propagate from seed, which is best extracted from the 'cones' with the aid of fire or a hot oven.

### Banksia integrifolia

**Coast banksia**

Of wide north–south distribution on the coast of eastern Australia, this salt-tolerant species forms at maturity a gnarled tree of up to 50 ft (15 m), with a trunk 18 in (45 cm) in diameter. Lime green flowers fading to dull yellow form cylindrical spikes about 4 in (10 cm) long from late summer to early winter. The distinctive silver-backed leaves, dull green above, are toothed only on young plants. In cultivation, this species makes remarkably rapid growth, especially in deep sandy soil. Zones 9–11.

### Banksia serrata

**Old man banksia, Saw banksia**

This species is distinguished by its gnarled appearance; it has a short crooked trunk, thick, wrinkled, fire-resistant bark, and leathery, saw-toothed leaves. Large, greenish-cream flower spikes appear from summer through autumn. The common name old man banksia derives from its bristly gray fruiting spikes, which have protruding fruit like small noses or chins. In its native southeastern Australia it grows on coastal dunes as well as sandstone ranges, reaching as much as 40 ft (12 m) in height; usually much smaller in cultivation, it is long-lived and moderately frost hardy. Zones 9–11.

## BETULA
*Birch*

These deciduous trees extend to the far northern regions of the globe as well as growing on the lower-latitude mountains of the northern hemisphere. Birches are among the most admired of all trees as landscape subjects, despite having fairly inconspicuous flowers and fruits. Their appeal lies in their sparkling white to pinkish-brown trunks, combined with vivid green spring foliage and a

Opposite: *Betula pendula*

*Betula papyrifera var. kenaica*     *Betula pendula*     *Betula utilis*

delicate tracery of winter twigs. The short, broad, serrated leaves mostly turn gold in autumn before dropping. Their fast early growth, yet fairly modest final height makes them ideal for use in gardens or streets. In the wild, birches often grow in dense stands rather than scattered among other trees.

## Cultivation

To grow birches successfully, a climate cool enough for at least the occasional winter snowfall is needed. Birches are shallow-rooted and need water during dry periods. They grow best in full sun or dappled shade in deep, well-drained soil, but some adapt to poorer, shallower, even boggy soil. Propagation is normally from the small winged seeds, produced in vast numbers from the cylindrical female catkins.

### Betula papyrifera

**Paper birch, Canoe birch**

Famed for its tough papery bark, once used by Native Americans for their light but strong canoes, the paper birch is one of the most wide-ranging North American species and is extremely cold hardy. It reaches 60 ft (18 m) in cultivation, and has a sparse crown. Its chief ornamental value is in the bark, which is white or cream and peels off in thin, curling layers, exposing new bark of a pale orange-brown. **Betula papyrifera var. kenaica** is a smaller-growing tree from southern Alaska. It is up to 40 ft (12 m) tall with slightly smaller leaves and fissured bark at the base of older trees. Zones 2–9.

### Betula pendula

**syns Betula alba, B. verrucosa**
**Silver birch, White birch**

The silver birch is the most common birch in northern Europe and also one of the most elegant species. It has smooth gray-white bark and fine arching branchlets bearing small shimmering leaves. It is the most widely cultivated birch, ideal as a windbreak and generally trouble free in terms of pests and diseases. It reaches around 30–50 ft (9–15 m) in temperate climates but can reach 70–80 ft (21–24 m). Many cultivars have been named, including '**Purpurea**' with rich, dark purple leaves, '**Laciniata**' (commonly misidentified as '**Dalecarlica**') with deeply incised leaves and weeping branches; '**Tristis**' with an erect trunk but weeping branchlets; and '**Youngii**' with growth like a weeping willow and no leading shoot, which requires grafting on a standard. Zones 2–9.

### Betula utilis

**Himalayan birch**

From the middle altitudes of the Himalayas, this up to 60 ft (18 m) tree has pale, smooth, peeling bark and a broadly domed crown. The leaves, dark green with paler undersides and irregularly toothed, are up to 3 in (8 cm) long. Most widely grown is **Betula utilis var. jacquemontii** with dazzling white or cream bark that peels in horizontal bands. Several clones of this variety with outstanding bark qualities have been named as cultivars. There are also forms with darker orange-brown bark. **B. u. var. occidentalis** normally has duller grayish white bark. '**Jermyns**' is a cultivar selected for the whiteness of its bark, uninterrupted by any darker markings or bands. Zones 7–9.

## CARPINUS

*Hornbeam*

The subtle beauty of hornbeams lies in their usually smoothly fluted trunks and limbs, their neatly veined, small, simple leaves that color attractively in autumn, and their bunches of dry, winged fruit hanging from the twigs. *Carpinus* is a small genus of catkin-bearing, deciduous trees scattered across cool-climate areas of the northern hemisphere. In foliage and fruits there is not a

*Carpinus betulus* 'Columnaris'

> The subtle beauty of hornbeams lies in their small, simple leaves that color attractively in autumn and the dry, winged fruit.

*Casuarina equisetifolia*

huge variation between the species, though overall size and growth habit are distinct for each. Most, and in particular the European *Carpinus betulus*, yield a timber that is exceptionally strong, hard and close grained; it is much used in the mechanism of pianos. Long-lived and often slow-growing, hornbeams are useful small to medium-sized trees for parks, streets and lawns.

## Cultivation

These grow best in well-drained, moderately fertile soil in a sunny or part-shaded position. Propagation is normally from seed except for certain named clones, which must be grafted.

### Carpinus betulus

#### Common hornbeam, European hornbeam

Ranging from Asia Minor across Europe to eastern England, this species can grow to 80 ft (24 m) although 30 ft (9 m) is an average garden height. It has a broad, rounded crown and pale gray bark, fairly smooth and often fluted. The ovate leaves are ribbed and serrated, downy when young, and change from dark green in summer to yellow in autumn. Inconspicuous flowers in early spring are followed by clusters of pale yellow winged fruit. It likes cool, moist conditions. '**Columnaris**' is a compact grower to 30 ft (9 m) high and 20 ft (6 m) wide; '**Fastigiata**' (syn. '**Pyramidalis**') develops into a taller, broadly conical tree. Zones 6–9.

## CASUARINA
*She-oak, Australian pine*

Members of this genus of evergreen trees earned the name Australian pine from their conifer-like appearance. There are 6 species of wide distribution in Australia, and about as many again in islands to the north. Many other species once placed here are now classified under *Allocasuarina* or *Gymnostoma*. Despite bearing only inconspicuous (male and female) flowers, casuarinas are graceful trees, fast-growing, tolerant of strong winds and adaptable, often to very dry conditions. Casuarina wood makes excellent firewood. They are grown as shade or amenity trees and are valued by some farmers for the shelter they provide for stock, while others maintain that they poison the ground; some nitrogen-fixing organisms do inhabit their roots and there is some evidence that compounds released from the fallen branchlets inhibit other plant growth.

## Cultivation

Plant in full sun in fertile, moist, well-drained soil. Water well during the growing period, less so in winter. Propagate from seed in spring or cuttings in mid- to late summer. Pruning is rarely necessary.

### Casuarina equisetifolia

#### Beach she-oak, Horsetail tree

This tree of around 40–60 ft (12–18 m) tall, depending on soil and exposure, has a short trunk and long, weeping, silvery gray branchlets. It grows naturally on beaches and exposed coastal headlands, being very resistant to salt-laden winds and tolerant of poor, sandy soil. It is not at all frost hardy. Reputedly one of the best fuelwood trees in the world, beach she-oak is also used for boatbuilding, house construction and furniture-making. It has the widest natural distribution of any casuarina, occurring on tropical seashores around most parts of the Pacific and Indian oceans. Zones 10–12.

## CATALPA
*Catalpa, Indian bean tree*

This genus consists of 11 species of fast-growing, deciduous trees from East Asia and North America. Catalpas

*Catalpa bignonioides*

*Catalpa bignonioides* 'Aurea'

*Cedrus deodara*

have large, ovate leaves in opposite pairs, sprays of showy, bell-shaped flowers at the end of the branches, and extraordinarily long, thin fruits that open to release quantities of very light, winged seeds. They can be beautiful trees with a dense canopy of luxuriant foliage but may look scrappy if exposed to cold or dry winds or if soil is poor. Some species yield valuable timber.

## Cultivation

Grow in moist, well-drained soil in a sunny but sheltered position. Propagate from seed in autumn or cuttings in late spring or summer, or by budding in late summer or grafting in winter.

### Catalpa bignonioides

**Southern catalpa**

From Florida west to Mississippi in the USA, this species grows along riverbanks and around swamp edges. A reasonably compact tree of 25–50 ft (8–15 m) with a rounded, irregularly shaped crown, it is cultivated as an ornamental tree for streets and parks. The heart-shaped leaves taper to a fine point and have downy undersides; they turn black before dropping in autumn. Sprays of 2 in (5 cm), white flowers with frilled edges and orange blotches and purple spots on their lower lips appear in summer. '**Aurea**' has lime-yellow leaves. Zones 5–10.

## CEDRUS

*Cedar*

This is a renowned genus of conifers belonging to the pine family; the 4 species are so similar that some botanists treat them as subspecies or varieties of a single species. All have needle-like leaves arranged in rosettes on the short but long-lasting lateral shoots, which arise from axils of the longer needles on stronger growths. The pollen cones, shaped like small bananas and up to 4 in (10 cm) long, release large clouds of pollen in early spring. The seed cones are broadly egg- or barrel-shaped, pale bluish or brownish; they eventually shatter to release seeds with broad papery wings. As cultivated trees the cedars are valued for the fine architectural effects of their branching, the texture and color of their foliage, and their vigorous growth.

## Cultivation

In appropriate climatic conditions these conifers are long-lived and trouble free, growing massive with age. They need full sun and well-drained, chalky soil. Propagation is normally from seed, though cuttings, layering and grafting are used for certain cultivars.

### Cedrus atlantica

syn. *Cedrus libani* subsp. *atlantica*
**Atlas cedar**

Native to the Atlas Mountains (*atlantica* is the adjectival form) of Morocco and Algeria, this tree in its younger stages has a neat, pyramidal shape with stiffly ascending branches, but with age it spreads into a broadly flat-topped tree with massive limbs up to 100 ft (30 m) or more high on good sites. The densely clustered needles are never more than 1 in (25 mm) long and vary from dark green to bluish, though it is mainly the bluish forms that are seen in gardens. This species prefers moderately cool climates. The collective cultivar name '**Glauca**' is used for selected seedling plants with bluish foliage. Zones 6–9.

### Cedrus deodara

**Deodar, Deodar cedar**

The deodar (its Indian name) occurs in the western Himalayas, reaching over 200 ft (60 m) in the wild, but is now almost extinct over much of its former range. In cultivation it makes fast early growth. The long leading shoots nod over slightly, and

*Cercis canadensis*

*Cercis siliquastrum* 'Alba'

smaller branches are quite pendulous. The foliage is a dark, slightly grayish green, with needles about 1½ in (35 mm) long on strong shoots. The deodar is at its best in milder, humid climates in deep soil, making luxuriant growth and reaching 30 ft (9 m) in about 10 years. The most popular cultivar is '**Aurea**', with golden branch tips. Zones 7–10.

## CERCIS
Judas tree, Redbud

This genus is made up of small, deciduous trees or shrubs from North America, Asia and southern Europe. Their profuse clusters of pea-like flowers, bright rose pink to crimson, line the bare branches in spring; even the neat pointed buds, slightly deeper in color, make an elegant display, hence the American name redbud. The handsome, heart-shaped to almost circular leaves follow, along with flat seed pods up to 4 in (10 cm) long.

## Cultivation

All 7 or 8 species are worth cultivating, though not all are easily obtained. They resent disturbance to their roots, especially transplanting. A sunny position suits them best and they thrive in hot, dry summer weather, as long as the soil moisture is adequate in winter and spring. They are easily propagated from seed, though growth is usually slow and it may take many years for them to become larger than shrub size.

### Cercis canadensis

**Eastern redbud**

Native to eastern and central USA, this tree can reach 40 ft (12 m) in the wild and is strikingly beautiful in flower. In gardens it rarely exceeds 12 ft (3.5 m), branching close to the ground. The leaves are heart-shaped with a distinct point, and appear after the flowers. The buds are deep rose, and the paler rose flowers are profuse and showy; flowering may continue from spring into early summer. '**Forest Pansy**' has purple-colored leaves. Zones 5–9.

### Cercis siliquastrum

**Judas tree, Love tree**

Native to regions close to the Mediterranean and Black Sea coasts, this tree seldom exceeds 25 ft (8 m), even after several decades. The leaves are slightly bluish-green with rounded tips, and the late spring flowers, larger and deeper pinkish magenta than in other species, arise in clusters on previous years' growths. It is the most reliable ornamental species in regions where winters are mild. Those forms having distinct flower coloration include the paler '**Alba**' and the deeper reddish '**Rubra**'. Zones 7–9.

## CHAMAECYPARIS
False cypress

In the nineteenth century botanists classified these conifers as *Cupressus* (true cypresses), and indeed the differences are slight—*Chamaecyparis* has its tiny branchlets more flattened with the scale-like leaves of two types, and the cones are smaller and release their seed earlier. Nearly all the 8 *Chamaecyparis* species occur in cooler, moister, more northerly regions in North America and eastern Asia, while true cypresses mostly occur further south and in drier regions. Several species have many cultivars, which feature colored foliage (usually gold, bluish or bronze); narrow, fastigiate, columnar or dwarf habit; bizarre foliage traits; or needle-like juvenile foliage.

## Cultivation

These frost-hardy trees grow well in a cool, moist climate; they respond with fast growth to deep, rich, well-drained soil and a sheltered position. Cultivars are easily propagated from cuttings; the typical tree forms from seed.

*Chamaecyparis lawsoniana* — *Chamaecyparis pisifera* 'Boulevard' — *Cinnamomum camphora*

### Chamaecyparis lawsoniana

**Port Orford cedar, Lawson cypress**

From the humid coastal forests of northwestern USA, this is the most widely planted member of the genus in its typical form, as well as having given rise to a larger number of cultivars than any other conifer species. Planted trees are up to 120 ft (36 m) tall with trunks up to 4 ft (1.2 m) in diameter, narrowly conical with pendulous side branches producing rippling curtains of bluish-green to deep green foliage. Over 180 cultivars are currently available and many more have been named. Zones 6–10.

### Chamaecyparis pisifera

**Sawara cypress, Sawara false cypress**

This vigorous Japanese species grows to 150 ft (45 m) in the wild. A broad, conical tree, the lower sides of the branchlets are strongly marked bluish-white and the tiny scale leaves on juvenile growth are quite prickly. The cultivars fall into 4 groups: the **Squarrosa Group**, the **Plumosa Group** (the largest group), the **Filifera Group** and the **Nana Group**. 'Squarrosa' itself is a broadly pyramidal small tree to 65 ft (20 m) with pale bluish-gray juvenile foliage that turns dull purple in winter. The Plumosa Group includes '**Plumosa**', a conical or columnar tree to 20 ft (6 m) with mid-green foliage, the leaves shorter and less prickly than 'Squarrosa'; and '**Plumosa Aurea**' with yellow-green foliage. Of the Filifera Group, the best known is '**Filifera Aurea**', a broadly pyramidal shrub of up to 10 ft (3 m); its bright gold and green foliage has flattened fans of branchlets mixed with elongated 'rat's tail' branchlets that arch gracefully.

## Cinnamomum

This genus of the laurel family consists of around 250 species of evergreen trees from tropical and subtropical Asia and Australasia with smooth, strongly veined leaves. Highly aromatic compounds are present in the leaves, twigs and bark of all species. The flowers are small and white or cream in delicate sprays and are followed by small fleshy berries containing a single seed. The bark of *Cinnamomum zeylanicum* yields the spice cinnamon; *C. cassia* provides the spice cassia used in drinks and sweets. *C. camphora* is a source of commercial camphor and used in China to make storage chests.

### Cultivation

Most species require tropical or subtropical conditions, with fairly high rainfall; only *C. camphora* is adaptable to warm-temperate climates. They do best in full sun or dappled shade in deep, free-draining soil with plentiful water in summer. Propagate from seed in autumn.

### Cinnamomum camphora

**Camphor laurel, Camphor tree**

Native to China, Taiwan and southern Japan, this fast-growing tree is known to reach 120 ft (36 m) in height with a rounded crown spreading to 50 ft (15 m) wide, but half this height is more usual in gardens. The short, solid trunk has scaly gray bark. The leaves, pinkish when young, turn pale green and finally deep green as they age. Widely grown as a shade tree in parks and gardens and as a street tree, it self-seeds freely and can become invasive in subtropical climates—in parts of east-coastal Australia it has become a serious pest. Zones 9–11.

## Clethra

A scattering of deciduous tree and shrub species across North America and eastern Asia, plus a larger number of evergreens in warmer climates, principally Southeast Asia, and one outlying species on the island of Madeira make up the 30

Opposite: *Cinnamomum camphora*

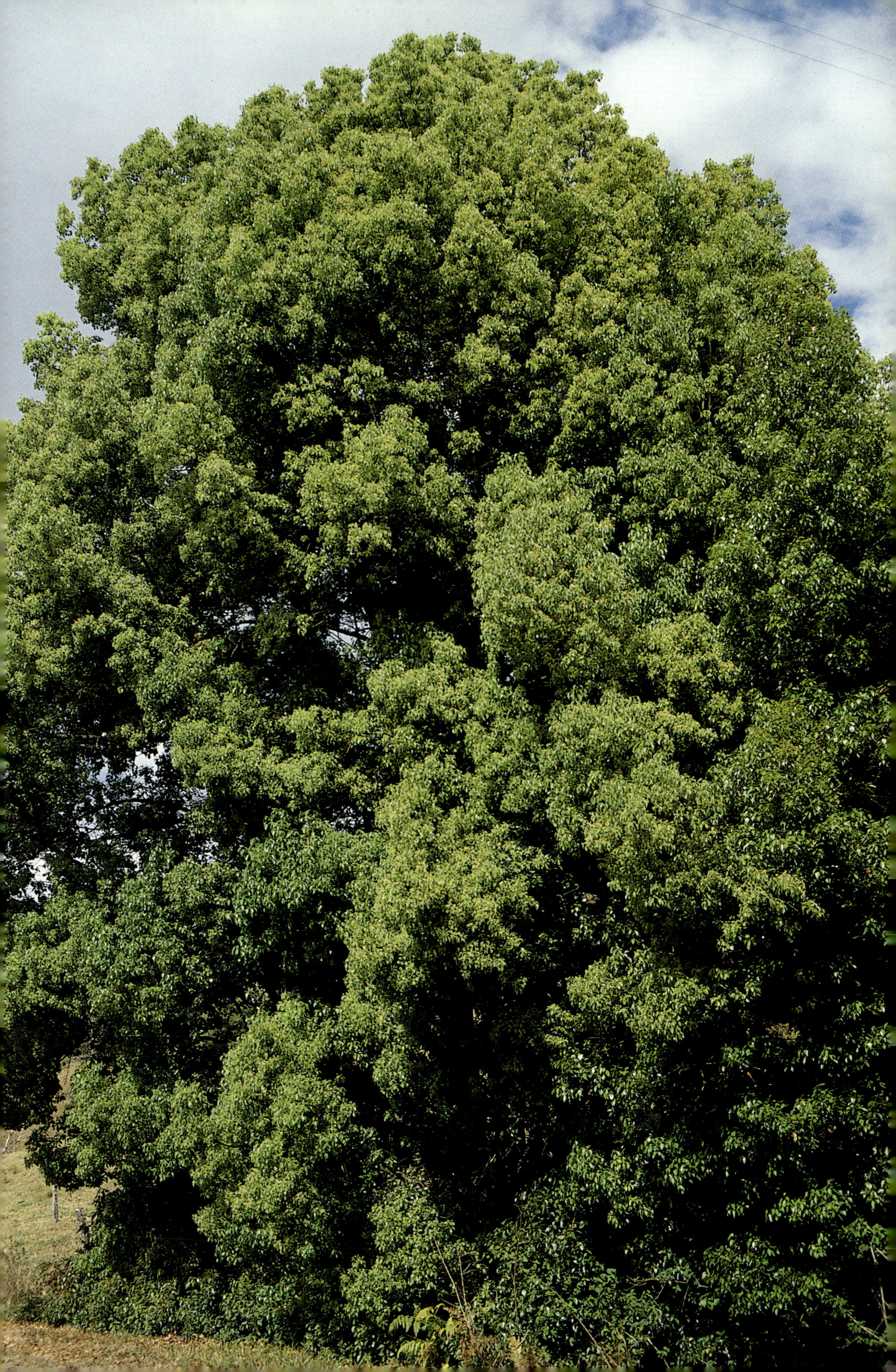

*Clethra arborea*

*Cornus capitata*

## TREES

species in this genus. The frost-hardy deciduous species mostly behave as spreading shrubs in cultivation, producing a thicket of stems concealed by dense foliage. The leaves are thin-textured with closely toothed margins. In summer and autumn small, white flowers are borne in delicate loose sprays, followed by numerous, tiny seed capsules.

### Cultivation

Clethras prefer sheltered, moist half-shaded spots and peaty, acid, moist but well-drained soil. Propagate from seed, cuttings or layers.

### Clethra arborea

**Lily-of-the-valley tree**

This species from Madeira requires milder conditions than others of the genus. An attractive densely leafed shrub or small tree 20–25 ft (6–8 m) tall, it has glossy leaves and long panicles of lily-of-the-valley-like flowers. Prune occasionally for shaping. Zones 9–10.

## CORDYLINE
Cabbage tree, Ti

Most species of this genus of 15 or so species of somewhat palm-like evergreen shrubs and small trees are tropical or subtropical, but a few are moderately frost hardy. Cordylines resemble dracaenas in habit and foliage, but differ in the flowers which are small and starry, borne in large panicles, and in the red, black or whitish fruits. Their underground rhizome, which sometimes emerges through the drainage apertures of a pot, appears to be for food storage.

### Cultivation

Cordylines do well in rich, well-drained soil. Narrower-leafed New Zealand species are the most sun hardy, and *Cordyline australis* tolerates salt spray near the ocean; the species with broader, thinner leaves prefer a sheltered position in part shade, though will tolerate full sun if humidity is high. Most can be kept in pots or tubs for many years as indoor or patio plants. They are easily propagated from seed or stem cuttings.

### Cordyline australis

syn. *Dracaena australis*
**New Zealand cabbage tree, Ti kouka**

This striking New Zealand native is moderately frost hardy, occurring in some of that country's southernmost areas. The seedlings, with very narrow, elegantly arching leaves, are sold as indoor plants and last for years in this juvenile state; planted outdoors they begin to form a trunk and the brownish-green leaves can be almost 3 ft (1 m) long and 2 in (5 cm) wide. The first large panicle of small white sweet-scented flowers, opening in summer, terminates the stem at a height of 6–8 ft (1.8–2.4 m); the stem then branches into several leaf rosettes, each in time flowering and branching again. It is the largest species, frequently reaching over 20 ft (6 m) tall with a stout trunk. '**Purpurea**' with bronze-purplish leaves is popular. '**Albertii**', a variegated cultivar with leaves striped cream, more pinkish on new growths, is less vigorous.
Zones 8–11.

## CORNUS
Cornel, Dogwood

About 45 species of shrubs, trees and even 1 or 2 herbaceous perennials make up this genus, widely distributed in temperate regions of the northern hemisphere. They include deciduous and evergreen species, all with simple, smooth-edged leaves that characteristically have prominent, inward-curving veins. The flowers are small, mostly greenish,

*Cordyline australis*

*Cornus controversa*

*Cornus mas*

yellowish or dull purplish: few are decorative, but in one group of species they are arranged in dense heads surrounded by large white, pink or yellow bracts that can be showy. Another shrubby group has stems and twigs that are often bright red or yellow, giving a decorative effect especially when leafless in winter. One such species is the common European dogwood, *Cornus sanguinea*. The fleshy fruits are also ornamental.

## Cultivation

The various species all do best in sun or very light shade. Most appreciate a rich, fertile, well-drained soil, though some of the multi-stemmed shrub species will grow well in boggy ground. Many are quite frost hardy but *Cornus capitata* will tolerate only light frosts. The species with decorative red stems can be cut back annually almost to ground level to encourage new growths, which have the best color. Propagate from seed or rooted layers struck in a moist sand-peat mixture.

### Cornus capitata

**syns *Benthamia fragifera*, *Dendrobenthamia capitata*
Himalayan strawberry tree, Evergreen dogwood, Bentham's cornus**

From the Himalayas and China, this evergreen dogwood makes a rounded, low-branched tree of 30 ft (9 m) after many years, with dense grayish-green foliage. In late spring and early summer its canopy is decked with massed flowerheads, each with 4 large bracts of a beautiful soft lemon yellow. In autumn it has large, juicy (but tasteless) scarlet compound fruit. Zones 8–10.

### Cornus controversa

**Table dogwood, Giant dogwood**

Native to China, Korea and Japan, this handsome deciduous species makes a tree of about 40 ft (12 m) with age, with a straight trunk and horizontal tiers of foliage. The glossy, strongly veined leaves are arranged alternately on the reddish twigs, a feature shared by *Cornus alternifolia* only. In bloom it is one of the showiest of the species lacking large bracts, with white flowers in flat clusters about 4 in (10 cm) across borne in early summer. The fruit is shiny black, and autumn foliage is red to purplish. '**Variegata**' has leaves with creamy white margins. Zones 6–9.

### Cornus florida

**Flowering dogwood**

Popular for its beauty and reliability, this species reaches 20 ft (6 m) or more tall with a single, somewhat crooked trunk, and in mid-spring bears an abundance of flowerheads, each with 4 large white or rose-pink bracts. In late summer the scattered red fruit makes a fine showing, and in autumn the foliage is scarlet and deep purple with a whitish bloom on the leaf undersides. *Cornus florida* prefers a warm summer and may not flower well in cool-summer climates. '**Rubra**' has dark rose bracts that are paler at the base. '**Apple Blossom**' has pale pink flower bracts. Zones 5–9.

### Cornus mas

**Cornelian cherry**

When it flowers in late winter or early spring on the leafless branches, this tree species looks unlike most other dogwoods. The flowers are tiny and golden yellow, grouped in small clusters without decorative bracts, but so profuse on the small twigs as well as on thicker branches that they make a fine display. Stiff and rather narrow at first, with maturity it becomes a spreading tree of 25 ft (8 m) or so. Edible fruit ripens bright red in late summer. Native to central and southeastern Europe, *Cornus mas* provides much-needed winter color for streets, parks and gardens. '**Variegata**' has white-margined leaves. Zones 6–9.

*Corymbia ficifolia*

*Crataegus laevigata* 'Paul's Scarlet'

> Hawthorns are robust, frost-hardy, deciduous trees, most of them compact enough even for quite small gardens.

## Corymbia

The 113 species of trees from Australia and Papua New Guinea that make up this newly recognized genus are still treated as 'eucalypts' in the broad sense. Mainly tropical, they comprise mostly the 'bloodwood' group of eucalypts with soft, crumbly or corky bark and cream, pink or red flowers carried in showy clusters at tips of branches—the spectacular red-flowering gum of Western Australia, *Corymbia ficifolia*, is a typical example. But just to confuse the issue, some 'bloodwoods' (in the botanical sense) have smooth bark, for example the well-known lemon-scented gum (*C. citriodora*).

### Cultivation

The species vary in their requirements and ease of cultivation. Many come from tropical regions with a short wet season and long dry season, and these rarely adapt well to more temperate climates. A number have proved more adaptable, though, and are popular in cultivation. They prefer full sun, and thrive in most soils, from heavy clay to light sand. All are drought tolerant once established. They are easily propagated from seed and should be planted in their permanent positions when not more than 24 in (60 cm) high.

### Corymbia ficifolia

syn. ***Eucalyptus ficifolia***
**Scarlet-flowering gum, Red-flowering gum**

This most spectacular eucalypt bears large terminal clusters of scarlet to orange flowers in late spring or summer, followed by large, urn-shaped fruit. (Forms with crimson or pink flowers are suspected of being hybrids of *E. calophylla*.) It grows to about 30 ft (9 m) with rough bark and a spreading crown of lance-shaped foliage. It performs best in a winter-rainfall climate. Zones 9–10.

## Crataegus
Hawthorn, May

Native to cool-climate areas of Europe, Asia and eastern North America, *Crataegus* belongs to the pome-fruit group of the rose family and the resemblance of the fruits to miniature apples can easily be seen and tasted. Most of the 200 species have long, sharp thorns on the summer growths; the leaves are either toothed or lobed, and the white or rarely pink flowers are clustered in flat to rounded umbels in late spring or summer. They are followed in autumn by a display of fruit mostly in shades of red, often also with attractive foliage colors.

### Cultivation

Hawthorns are robust, frost-hardy, deciduous trees, most of them compact enough even for quite small gardens. They are sun-lovers and not very fussy about soil type or drainage. Some species sucker from the base, but suckers can be removed to produce a tree form. Some hawthorns are prone to fireblight, controlled only by prompt removal and burning of affected branches. Foliage may also be disfigured by the 'pear and cherry slug' (larva of a sawfly); spray severe attacks with an insecticide. Propagate from cold-stratified seed, or by grafting of named clones. In winter they are easily transplanted.

### Crataegus laevigata

syn. ***Crataegus oxyacantha***
**Midland hawthorn, May, English hawthorn**

This small tree reaches 25 ft (8 m) or more in height and spread. Native to Europe and North Africa, it is easily confused with the English may (*Crataegus monogyna*). It has mid- to dark green, glossy leaves with shallow, rounded lobes and produces few thorns. Abundant white flowers open in late spring. Cultivar '**Paul's Scarlet**' has bright

*Crataegus × lavallei*

*Cryptomeria japonica*

crimson double flowers in late spring; **'Punicea'** has deep pink single flowers with white centers; **'Punicea Flore Pleno'** is similar but with double flowers. Zones 4–9.

### Crataegus × lavallei

**syn.** *Crataegus × carrierei*
**Lavalle hawthorn, Carriere hawthorn**

This hybrid originated in France in about 1880, the result of a cross between *Crataegus crus-galli* and *C. pubescens*. A densely branched, almost thornless tree of 15–20 ft (4.5–6 m), the broad, irregularly toothed leaves are darker glossy green than most hawthorns and are semi-evergreen in warmer climates. The white flowers with red stamens open in loose clusters in early summer, then large yellow fruit ripens to orange-red. Its autumn foliage tones intensify after the first hard frost. Zones 6–10.

## CRYPTOMERIA

*Japanese cedar, sugi*

One species is accepted in this conifer genus from China and Japan, though there are many variations. Often fast-growing, the branches and branchlets of this evergreen are clothed in short, leathery needle leaves that are densely overlapping and curve inward slightly. Male (pollen) and female (seed) cones are on the same tree, the former in profuse clusters and releasing clouds of pollen in spring, the latter in sparser groups behind the branch tips. Its handsome shape and uniformity of growth make it highly suitable for windbreaks, hedges and avenues. In Japan it is grown for its timber, but is also venerated in historic groves.

### Cultivation

Very frost hardy, it prefers full sun or part-shade and deep, fertile, moist but well-drained soil. It likes plenty of water. Propagation is from seed, or from cuttings for the cultivars.

### Cryptomeria japonica

This species can grow 20–25 ft (6–8 m) in 10 years; old trees in Japan are up to 150 ft (45 m) high, with massive trunks. The thick, brown bark has straight, vertical furrows. Growth habit is conical with a long, pointed leader. The Japanese race has thicker branchlets and stiffer habit than the Chinese one, ***Cryptomeria japonica* var. *sinensis***. There are at least 50 cultivars, most dwarf but not all. Best known of the taller ones is **'Elegans'**, which makes a solid column of foliage to 30 ft (9 m) high and 8 ft (2.4 m) across; needles are long and soft; in winter the tree turns a striking dull bronze or plum color. Zones 7–10.

## × CUPRESSOCYPARIS

The '×' in front of the name indicates that this is a bigeneric hybrid, that is, a hybrid between 2 different genera, in this case *Cupressus* and *Chamaecyparis*. Although the name applies to any hybrid between these genera (including later generations and backcrosses), it is best known in the form of the one which first appeared in England in 1888 as a chance hybrid between the frost-hardy *Chamaecyparis nootkatensis* and the less hardy *Cupressus macrocarpa*. Two additional hybrids have since been raised, their *Cupressus* parents being *C. glabra* and *C. lusitanica* respectively.

### Cultivation

These conifers combine rapid growth with reasonable frost-hardiness, and adapt well to poorly drained soil but not to arid climates. They are widely planted for fast-growing hedges as they respond well to frequent trimming. However, if they are left untrimmed they rapidly grow to tree size. Propagate from cuttings, which strike readily under nursery conditions. Although seed is fertile, the resulting seedlings might vary.

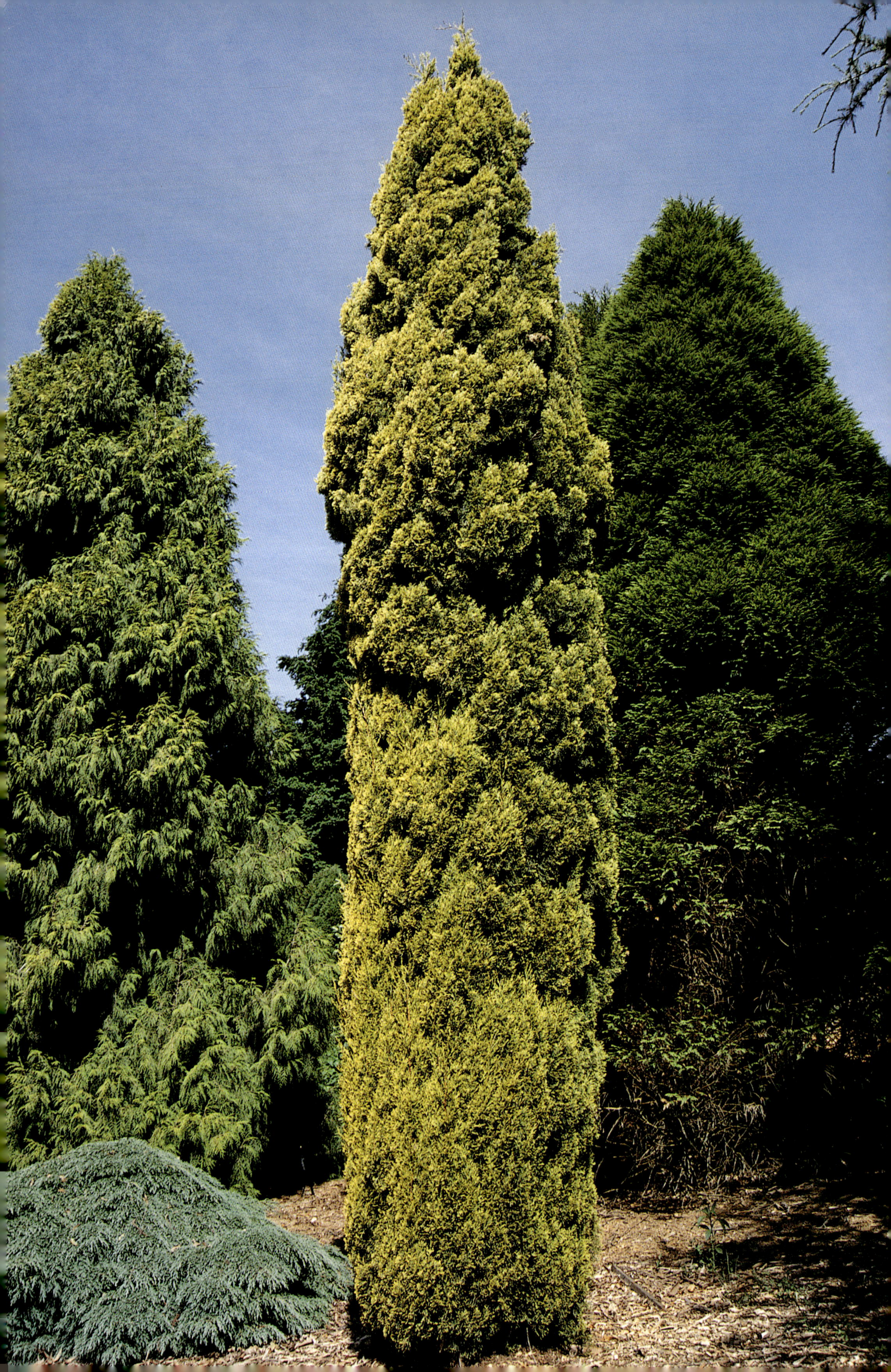

*Cupressus macrocarpa* 'Aurea'

*Cupressus cashmeriana*

*Cupressus sempervirens* 'Gracilis'

## × *Cupressocyparis leylandii*

**Leyland cypress**

Representing the original cross between *Chamaecyparis nootkatensis* and *Cupressus macrocarpa*, this name encompasses a number of seedling clones, some of which have been named as cultivars. When used without specifying a cultivar name it usually refers to '**Haggerston Gray**' or '**Leighton Green**', which both make very vigorous, upright trees with a long, open leading shoot and slightly irregular outline; foliage is deep green or slightly grayish. In good soil it will reach 30 ft (9 m) in 10 years and double that in 30 years, ultimately growing to 100 ft (30 m) or more. '**Naylor's Blue**' has more strongly bluish-green foliage and is more columnar in habit. Zones 5–10.

## CUPRESSUS

*Cypress*

This conifer genus has been cultivated since classical times but species are seldom planted where winters are severe due to limited cold tolerance. Most of the 20 or so species occur wild in western USA, Mexico and Guatemala. As well as the wild forms the cypresses include many cultivars. These handsome ornamentals come in many foliage hues; they range from tall to dwarf, from columnar to weeping or high-crowned and spreading. Dense foliage and rapid growth makes them useful screens and windbreaks.

## Cultivation

Some species are very tolerant of dry conditions, others need a moister climate. Soil and sunlight requirements vary; generally they prefer full sun, well-drained soil and protection from cold winds. They are easy to propagate from seed, and cultivars are almost as easily raised from cuttings. Some cypress species suffer from cypress canker, which disfigures trees and finally kills them.

## *Cupressus cashmeriana*

**Kashmir cypress**

Despite its name, this species is not native to Kashmir but to Bhutan. It should by rights be called 'Bhutan cypress', except that *Cupressus torulosa* has a prior claim to this common name. This beautiful cypress has long, weeping sprays of blue-green, aromatic foliage, but is difficult to grow. In a suitable warm, moist climate it grows fast at first, attaining 20–30 ft (6–9 m) in 15 years, but is easily damaged by wind and may die in hot or dry spells. Some fine specimens grow in cooler mountain areas of the wet tropics, and it does well in wetter hill areas of the Mediterranean, the western USA, eastern Australia and New Zealand. Zones 9–11.

## *Cupressus macrocarpa*

**Monterey cypress**

Endemic to a very short stretch of the central Californian coast near Monterey, this grows into one of the largest of all cypresses, reaching 120 ft (36 m) tall with a trunk diameter of 8 ft (2.4 m). When planted in a grove it forms a tall, straight trunk, but in the open in good soil it branches low with massive, spreading limbs, producing a broad, dense crown of deep green with a rather spiky outline. Close up, the foliage is rather coarse, and it has a slightly sour smell when bruised. The cones are large and wrinkled. It grows best in cool but mild climates with winter rainfall and takes only 10 years or so to form a dense 30–40 ft (9–12 m) tree. It is one of the most popular farm hedging trees in New Zealand. Several golden foliaged cultivars are available. Zones 7–10.

## *Cupressus sempervirens*

**Funereal cypress, Italian cypress, Mediterranean cypress**

This species, familiar in Italy, France and Spain, came from the eastern Mediterranean. It has fine

Opposite: *Cupressus sempervirens*

*Davidia involucrata*

*Davidia involucrata*

## 44
### TREES

dark grayish-green foliage with very tiny scale leaves in slightly flattened sprays, and large, slightly elongated, pale brown cones. In its growth habit the Mediterranean cypress exhibits a curious phenomenon: the form usually cultivated, known as '**Stricta**', is narrowly columnar, but a proportion of its seedlings grow into trees with side branches at a wide angle to the trunk; this form is often known as '**Horizontalis**'. More tolerant of dry conditions and slower growing than most cypresses, it makes quite vigorous growth under good conditions in a warm climate. The '**Stricta**' form can reach 15–20 ft (4.5–6 m) in 10 years, often as a slim column at this stage, but old trees of 30–40 ft (9–12 m) are usually much broader. '**Swane's Golden**', an Australian cultivar with foliage flecked golden yellow with deeper gold tips, can reach 20 ft (6 m) or more. '**Gracilis**' is a narrowly columnar cultivar raised in New Zealand, slow-growing and maturing at about 15 ft (4.5 m) with a width of about 3 ft (1 m). Zones 8–10.

## DAVIDIA

*Dove tree, Handkerchief tree*

Native to western China, this genus contains just one species, though some varieties occur. In China, it can reach over 60 ft (18 m), with a rounded crown, and in full flower it is one of the most striking of all deciduous trees outside the tropics. 'Like huge butterflies hovering' is how plant explorer E. H. Wilson described the long-stalked flowerheads, each nestled between 2 large, drooping white or cream bracts. The surface of the large, soft, toothed leaves is deeply creased by veins.

### Cultivation

The tree is frost hardy, but the bracts need protecting from wind. It needs rich, porous soil and full sun or part-shade. Propagate from the whole fruit, which may take up to 3 years to germinate. Cold treatment assists germination.

### *Davidia involucrata*

This conical tree has broad leaves up to 6 in (15 cm) long, and small, deep-set, brownish-red flowers surrounded by 2 white bracts of unequal lengths. The greenish-brown, pendent, ridged fruit are up to 2 in (5 cm) across. The more common cultivated form is ***Davidia involucrata* var. *vilmoriniana***, which has paler and less downy leaf undersides. Zones 7–9.

## ERIOBOTRYA

This genus, which belongs to the rose family, includes 30 species of evergreen shrubs and trees. Only the loquat, *Eriobotrya japonica*, is commonly grown. Widely distributed through eastern Asia, from the eastern Himalayas to Japan, they include trees growing to 30 ft (9 m). All types bear leathery, deeply veined leaves with silvery or felty undersides. The creamy white, scented flowers are held in loose sprays at the tips of the branches during autumn, and are followed by edible, decorative fruits.

### Cultivation

Easily grown, they are marginally frost hardy and will tolerate dry as well as coastal conditions. Grow in a fertile, well-drained soil in a sunny position. Propagate from seed or cuttings in early summer.

### *Eriobotrya japonica*

**Loquat**

Native to China and Japan, the loquat can grow to 20–30 ft (6–9 m) tall. It forms a shapely conical tree, but in gardens it can be kept considerably more compact if pruned after the golden-yellow

*Davidia involucrata*

*Loquats are easy to grow in a fertile, well-drained soil in a sunny position.*

*iobotrya japonica*

*Erythrina crista-galli*

fruit have been harvested. The large, deep green leaves are pale and felty underneath. *Eriobotrya japonica* blooms in late autumn and the fruit, which set in winter, ripen in spring. It is very susceptible to fruit fly, and birds can also damage the crop. This is a plant for temperate areas where ample moisture is available as the fruit mature. Zones 8–10.

## Erythrina
*Coral tree*

The 108 species of deciduous and semi-evergreen trees and shrubs in this genus occur wild in tropical and subtropical regions around the world, though with most species in the Americas and Africa. Belonging to the bean tribe of the legumes, they are grown as ornamentals for their vividly hued flowers. Their trunks and branches are protected by short, sharp prickles; many species have weak branches that tend to fall in storms. The leaves are compound with 3 broad, often diamond-shaped leaflets. Bean-like flowers in scarlet, crimson or orange are borne in racemes towards the ends of the branches at varying times of the year (some species in mid-winter), followed by narrow seed pods that dry and brown as they ripen.

## Cultivation

Most species are not frost hardy, but some are happy enough in exposed coastal locations. They all enjoy full sun and well-drained soil. Spider mites may be a problem. Propagation is from seed in spring or cuttings in summer.

### Erythrina caffra

**syns** *Erythrina constantiana, E. insignis*
**South African coral tree, Kaffirboom**

This semi-evergreen tree with a broad, open crown quickly reaches about 30–60 ft (9–18 m) and is often grown as a shade tree in its native South Africa. The compound leaves, 6 in (15 cm) wide, have 3 broad leaflets. From late spring to early summer clusters of pale orange to orange-red flowers are borne on almost bare branches (sometimes quite thorny). The cultivar '**Flavescens**' has pale cream flowers and is equally attractive. Zones 9–11.

### Erythrina crista-galli

**Common coral tree, Cock's comb**

This species from South America is the best known coral tree in temperate climates, where it is treated almost as an herbaceous plant, being cut back almost to the ground in autumn after flowering, transferred to a large pot and overwintered under glass. It is also grown permanently in the greenhouse and again pruned severely in late autumn. It grows about 6 ft (1.8 m) tall under these conditions. In subtropical climates it grows into a gnarled, wide-crowned tree 15–30 ft (4.5–9 m) tall and bears its scarlet or coral-red flowers in spring and summer. Zones 8–11.

## Eucalyptus
*Eucalypt, Gum tree*

Australia is the original home of all but a few of over 700 species that make up this genus of evergreen trees of the myrtle family. Beyond Australia, a handful of species are native to southern New Guinea, southeastern Indonesia, and the southern Philippines. But eucalypts are possibly the world's most widely planted trees, especially in drier subtropical and tropical regions, for example in Africa, the Middle East, India and South America. They are renowned for their fast height growth and ability to thrive on poor or degraded land, providing shelter, timber and fuel, though they may create environments hostile to other plants and animals of importance in traditional rural culture.

Eucalypts are unusual trees, with leaves that

*Eucalypts are possibly the world's most widely planted trees.*

Eucalyptus nicholii

Eucalyptus pauciflora

tend to hang vertically so foliage provides only partial shade; the leaves contain aromatic oil in small translucent cavities, eucalyptus oil being an important product of certain species. The nectar-rich flowers are abundant, mostly white, but yellow, pink or red in a minority of species, with the massed stamens the most conspicuous part. Petals and sepals are fused into a cap-like structure (operculum) that is shed as the stamens unfold; fruit is woody capsules, mostly quite small. The bark of many eucalypts is smooth and shed annually, and the new and old bark can make a colorful contrast while this is happening.

## Cultivation

There are species to suit most climates except those where winter temperatures fall below about 10°F (−12°C), but the great majority of species will tolerate only the lightest frosts. Drought hardiness also varies greatly, some species requiring fairly moist conditions. With rare exceptions eucalypts are grown from seed, which germinates freely. They should be planted out into the ground when no more than 18 in (45 cm) high, ensuring that roots have not coiled in the container at any stage. They seldom survive transplanting, and are not long-lived as container plants. They prefer full sun at all stages of growth.

### Eucalyptus leucoxylon

**Yellow gum, South Australian blue gum, White ironbark**

A tree from high rainfall regions of South Australia, this shapely eucalypt grows to 100 ft (30 m) with an open canopy. Its distinctive bark is fissured at the base but smooth and dappled with yellowish-white and blue-gray spots above. The leaves are grayish or bluish-green and taper to a point. The large, 1½ in (35 mm) wide flowers, which may be cream or dark pink, are borne in small clusters. Crimson-flowering plants may be sold as ***Eucalyptus leucoxylon* 'Rosea'**. Zones 9–11.

### Eucalyptus nicholii

**Narrow-leafed black peppermint, Willow leaf peppermint**

This fibrous-barked species from the highlands of northeastern New South Wales makes an excellent shade or street tree. Its white flowers can only be appreciated when the tree is small. The fine, sickle-shaped, blue-green leaves are held aloft on a high crown. Withstanding mild frosts and strong winds, it grows to 40–50 ft (12–15 m). Zones 8–11.

### Eucalyptus pauciflora

**syn. *Eucalyptus coriacea***
**Snow gum**

This 30–60 ft (9–18 m) tree is found in southeastern Australia, commonly growing in frost-prone highland valleys. It tends to have a rather twisted trunk, with reddish-brown or gray bark peeling in irregular strips to reveal white and beige under-bark. Small cream flowers are borne in spring and summer. Alpine snow gum, ***Eucalyptus pauciflora* subsp. *niphophila*** (syn. *E. niphophila*), occurs at altitudes over 5,000 ft (1,500 m) where snow lies through most of winter; it is smaller and lower branching. Zones 7–9.

### Eucalyptus torquata

**Coral gum**

This small Western Australian tree grows to 20 ft (6 m) with a fairly narrow, upright habit. Its blue-green, sickle-shaped leaves are 4 in (10 cm) long, and the rough brown bark flakes rather than peels. Orange-red, lantern-shaped buds, 1 in (25 mm) long, open to a mass of creamy orange and yellow or pink and yellow stamens, followed by large seed capsules. It can withstand dry conditions but does better with regular moisture. Zones 9–11.

*Eucalyptus torquata*      *Eucryphia cordifolia*      *Fagus sylvatica*

## EUCRYPHIA

This small genus of about 6 species is made up of evergreen or semi-deciduous trees from the southern hemisphere. All species have pure white flowers of singular beauty, rather like small single roses with 4 petals and a 'boss' of red-tipped stamens. There are 2 species indigenous to Chile and 4 indigenous to Australia. Eucryphias have been grown in the British Isles for more than a century, especially in mild, moist, Atlantic coastal districts where the climate suits them well. Several garden hybrids are more vigorous and floriferous than the species.

### Cultivation
Frost hardy, they require a humid microclimate and constant soil moisture combined with good drainage. Good flowering demands that the tree crown be in the sun but the roots shaded. Propagate from seed or cuttings in summer.

### *Eucryphia cordifolia*

**Ulmo**

Growing to a medium to large tree in the wettest coastal rainforests of southern Chile, this tree was called 'ulmo' (meaning elm) by the Spanish settlers. The simple, oblong, wavy-edged, shiny dark green leaves are gray beneath. White flowers 2 in (5 cm) across are borne singly in late summer. In cultivation this evergreen species has proved more tender than the others and, while its foliage is interesting with reddish new growths, it is not very free flowering. In very mild, wet climates it grows tall and slender, up to 20–25 ft (6–8 m) in under 10 years. Zones 9–11.

## FAGUS
*Beech*

Although these long-lived, deciduous trees, to 130 ft (40 m), are scattered across Europe, the UK, Asia and North America, most of the 10 species are confined to China and Japan. They are absent from far northern forests as well as lowland Mediterranean-type forests. Most species have a rounded crown of delicate foliage that turns golden brown in autumn, and smooth, gray bark. They bear brown-scaled, pointed winter buds and prominently veined ovate to elliptic leaves. In spring new leaves are briefly accompanied by small, individual clusters of male and female flowers. In early autumn, small shaggy fruit capsules split open to release angular, oil-rich seeds (beech nuts) that are a major food source for wildlife. Their valuable timber is close-grained and readily worked; it is used for flooring, furniture and making kitchen utensils.

### Cultivation
Frost hardy, beeches require well-drained, reasonably fertile soil and some shelter from strong wind; they do best in areas with long, warm summers. Purple-leafed forms prefer full sun and yellow-leafed forms a little shade. Propagate from fresh seed; cultivars must be grafted. They are prone to attack by aphids and powdery mildew.

### *Fagus sylvatica*

**Common beech, European beech**

Although regarded as an 'English' native, this species ranges across Europe and western Asia. Growing to about 80 ft (24 m), it bears drooping balls of yellowish male flowers and greenish clusters of female flowers in spring. Cultivars selected for their habit, intricately cut leaves and colorful foliage include '**Aspleniifolia**'; '**Dawyck**' with a narrow columnar habit to 50 ft (15 m) and dark purple foliage; '**Pendula**' with branches that droop from a mushroom-shaped crown; *Fagus sylvatica* **f. *purpurea*** (syn. '**Atropunicea**'), a round-headed copper beech with purple-green leaves that turn copper; '**Riversii**', the purple beech, with very dark purple leaves; '**Rohanii**' with brownish-purple deeply cut leaves; '**Rotundifolia**' with strong

*Fraxinus angustifolia*

*Fraxinus escelsior* 'Pendula'

upright growth and small rounded leaves; '**Tricolor**' (syn. '**Roseomarginata**'), a smaller tree with purplish leaves edged and striped pink and cream; and '**Zlatia**' with yellow young foliage turning green. Zones 5–9.

## Fraxinus
Ash

This genus of 65 mainly deciduous, fast-growing tree species ranges throughout the northern hemisphere except for the coldest regions and lowland tropics. Unlike other woody members of the olive family (Oleaceae) it has pinnate leaves consisting of several leaflets, small insignificant flowers that in most species lack petals, and single-seeded, winged fruits called samaras. One group, the 'flowering ashes', typified by *Fraxinus ornus*, produces showier flowers with small petals in large terminal panicles at the tips of branches. Some large species are valued for their tough, pale timber.

## Cultivation

Ashes are mostly quite frost hardy and can survive exposed or arid conditions, but thrive in shelter with fertile, moist but well-drained soil. Widely planted as street and park trees, they are seldom affected by pests or diseases. Propagate from seed in autumn; for cultivars, graft onto seedling stock of the same species.

### Fraxinus angustifolia

syn. *Fraxinus oxycarpa*
Narrow-leafed ash

This species is related to *Fraxinus excelsior*, with similar foliage, flowers and fruit but darker bark and leaves in whorls of 3 to 4, not in pairs. It can grow in semi-arid climates and has a broadly columnar to rounded crown. **F. a. subsp. *oxycarpa*** (the desert ash), has leaves with up to 7 leaflets, hairy under the midribs. '**Raywood**', apparently a clone of subspecies *oxycarpa*, is called the claret ash for its wine-colored autumn foliage. Zones 6–10.

### Fraxinus excelsior

European ash, Common ash

One of Europe's largest deciduous trees, this species can reach 140 ft (42 m); in the open it is usually 50–60 ft (15–18 m), with a broad crown. It bears dark green leaves with 9 to 11 narrow, toothed leaflets that turn yellow in autumn. Velvety, blackish flower buds are noticeable in winter. '**Aurea**' and the more vigorous '**Jaspidea**' have pale yellowish green summer foliage that deepens in autumn; the twigs turn yellow in winter. '**Pendula**', the weeping ash, has branches often weeping to the ground. Zones 4–10.

## Ginkgo
Ginkgo, Maidenhair tree

The Ginkgoales, seed-bearing plants more primitive than the conifers and more ancient, first appeared in the Permian Period (about 300 million years ago) and flourished through the Jurassic and Cretaceous Periods. About 100 million years ago they began to die out, leaving the maidenhair tree a sole survivor— and then only in China. It is now unknown in a wild state, and probably would no longer exist if ancient trees had not been preserved in temple grounds and young ones planted there. The common name 'maidenhair' refers to the leaf shape and vein pattern, resembling some of the maidenhair fern (*Adiantum*) species. Male trees bear small spikes of pollen sacs, females solitary naked seeds ('fruits') with an oily flesh around the large kernel.

## Cultivation

A tree of temperate climates, it resists pollution and seems to have outlived any pests it may have once had. It does, however, need shelter from strong winds and does best in deep, fertile soil.

**Opposite:** *Ginkgo biloba*

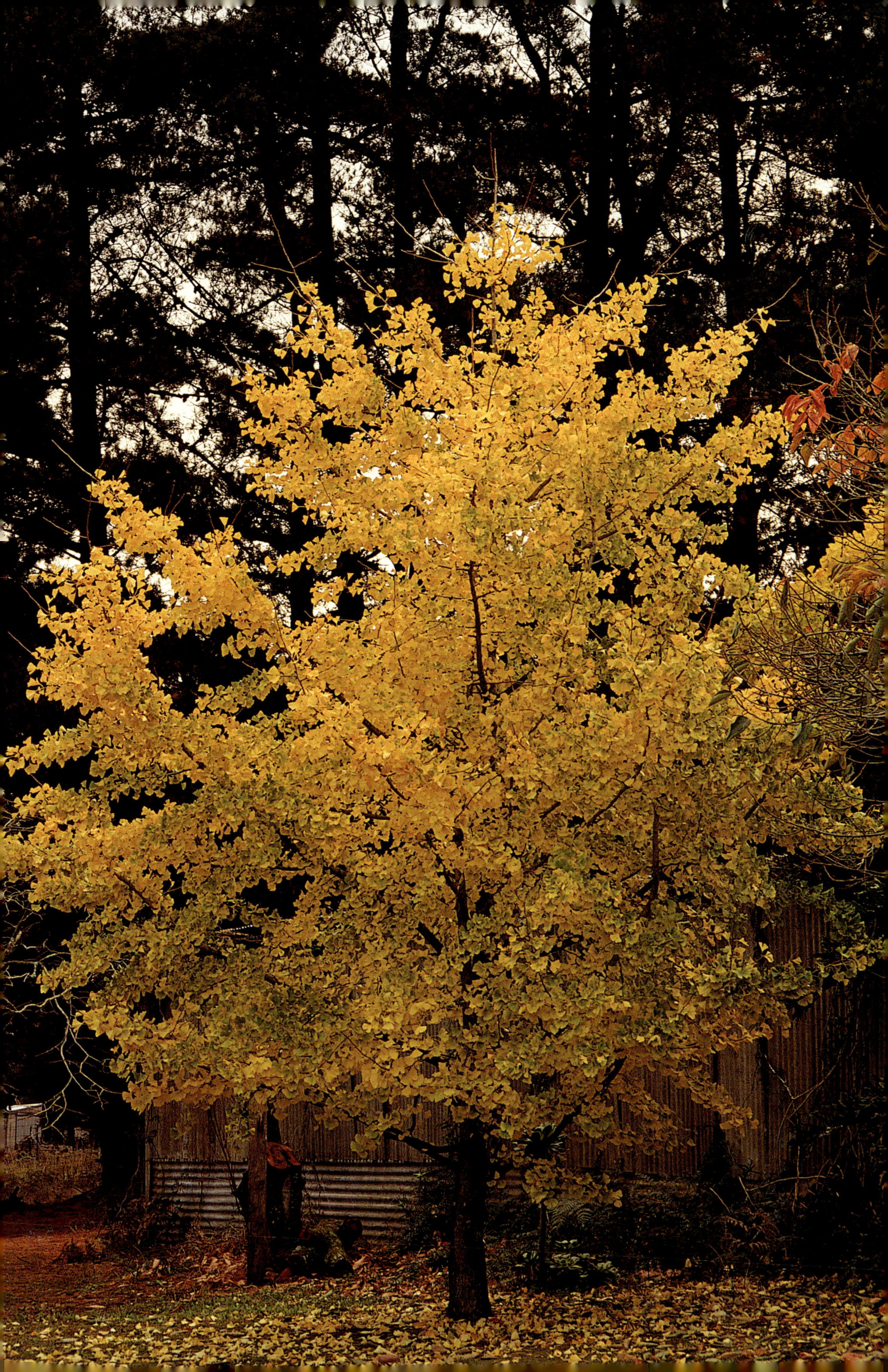

*Gleditsia triacanthos* 'Skyline'

City authorities prefer to grow male trees, as females drop smelly fruit; in China female trees are preferred as the seeds are edible and nutritious. Fruit does not appear before the tree is at least 20 years old, however. Propagate from seed or autumn cuttings.

### Ginkgo biloba

The ginkgo grows at least 80 ft (24 m) tall, upright when young and eventually spreading to 30 ft (9 m) or more. Deciduous, the 4 in (10 cm) long, matt green, fan-shaped leaves turn golden yellow in autumn. A fleshy, plum-like orange-brown fruit with an edible kernel appears in late summer and autumn if male and female trees are grown together. '**Fastigiata**' is a slender, erect cultivar that reaches 30 ft (9 m). '**Princeton Sentry**' has a narrow, upright habit and is male. Zones 3–10.

## GLEDITSIA

Locust

Occurring in temperate and subtropical regions of North and South America as well as Africa and Asia, this genus of about 14 species of deciduous, broadly spreading, usually thorny trees is grown for attractive foliage, ease of cultivation and for shade. They have pinnate or bipinnate leaves, inconspicuous flowers and large, often twisted, hanging seed pods that are filled with a sweetish, edible pulp. The locust referred to in the Bible is the related *Ceratonia siliqua*, but in North America 'locust' has been used for both *Gleditsia* and *Robinia*, the latter not closely related.

## Cultivation

Gleditsias grow best in full sun in rich, moist soil and tolerate poor drainage. They are fast-growing and mostly frost hardy, although young plants may need protection from frost. Prune young trees to promote a single, straight trunk; thorns on the lower trunk can be removed. Propagate selected forms by budding in spring or summer and species from seed in autumn.

### Gleditsia triacanthos

**Honey locust**

Native to eastern and central USA and reaching 100 ft (30 m), this species has an open, vase-shaped canopy and a thorny trunk. Fern-like, shiny green bipinnate leaves with small leaflets turn deep yellow in autumn. Twisted black pods, up to 18 in (45 cm) long and $1\frac{1}{2}$ in (35 mm) wide, hang from the branches in autumn and winter. ***Gleditsia triacanthos* f. *inermis*** is thornless as are most modern cultivars. '**Imperial**' has rounded leaves and few seed pods; '**Ruby Lace**' has reddish young growth turning bronze in autumn; '**Shademaster**' is fast-growing and broadly conical with bright green leaves; '**Skyline**' has dark green leaves that turn yellow in autumn; '**Stevens**' is wide-spreading with bright green leaves turning yellow in autumn; and '**Sunburst**' has bright yellow young leaves that turn pale green in summer. Zones 3–10.

## GORDONIA

This genus of about 70 species of evergreen trees and shrubs allied to *Camellia* is native to Southeast Asia, except for one North American species. Their handsome, white-petalled camellia-like flowers and glossy, dark green leaves make them popular ornamental plants for warm climates.

## Cultivation

They do best in sun or dappled shade in friable, slightly acid soil—they enjoy conditions similar to those preferred by camellias. Mulch, feed and water regularly. Tip pruning during the first few

*Gleditsia triacanthos* 'Shademaster'

*The glossy, toothed leaves of Hoheria populnea resemble those of a poplar.*

Gordonia axillaris

Hoheria populnea

years of growth will improve their slightly open habit. Propagate from seed in autumn or spring, or from cuttings in late summer.

### Gordonia axillaris

Though it may become a tree up to 25 ft (8 m) tall and wide, this beautiful evergreen from China with dappled orange-brown bark grows slowly, and is usually seen as a tall shrub. The dark green, glossy leaves to 6 in (15 cm) long turn scarlet before they fall, a few at a time, throughout the year. The white flowers are about 4 in (10 cm) wide with broad, crumpled petals and golden stamens. Zones 9–11.

## HOHERIA

This genus consists of 5 species of evergreen and deciduous small trees native to the forests of New Zealand. Of slender, upright habit, they are grown for their showy clusters of faintly perfumed white flowers which appear in summer and autumn. Plants can be anywhere between 20–50 ft (6–15 m) high, and flowering is usually followed by the appearance of fruit capsules.

## Cultivation

Happiest in warm-temperate climates with high summer rainfall, they grow in sun or semi-shade in fertile, well-drained soil. Prune straggly plants by about one-third in winter; all plants benefit from a light annual pruning of the outer branches to maintain a tidy shape and abundant foliage. Propagate from seed in autumn or from cuttings in summer.

### Hoheria populnea

**Houhere, New Zealand lacebark**

This fast-growing evergreen tree forms a slender dome about 20 ft (6 m) high. Glistening white, 5-petalled flowers with golden-yellow stamens are borne in profuse clusters on young shoots in late summer and early autumn; winged fruit capsules follow. The glossy, toothed leaves resemble those of a poplar. Mature trees have distinctive, often flaky, pale brown and white bark. Zones 9–11.

## HYMENOSPORUM

*Australian frangipani, sweetshade*

This genus consists of a single species of evergreen tree originating in the subtropical rainforests of east coast Australia and New Guinea. It has showy tubular flowers and oval to oblong, glossy leaves. The name comes from the Greek *hymen*, a membrane, and *sporos*, a seed, referring to the winged seeds.

## Cultivation

A relatively fast-growing tree, it adapts to most soil types but prefers moist, humus-rich soil where it is less likely to be checked by long dry spells. It flowers best in a sheltered position in full sun, but will tolerate some shade. Propagation is easily done from seed or from cuttings.

### Hymenosporum flavum

Growing to 30 ft (9 m), taller in the wild, this tree has a straight, smooth trunk and open, columnar shape, with widely spaced horizontal branches and dark green glossy leaves clustered towards the ends. In spring it bears clusters of very fragrant cream flowers that age over several days to deep golden yellow. They are followed by flattish seed pods with small, winged seeds. Zones 9–11.

## IDESIA

*Wonder tree, Ligiri*

This genus consists of one species of deciduous tree. Indigenous to central and western China, Korea, Japan and neighboring islands, it is grown

TREES

*Idesia polycarpa*

*Ilex × altaclerensis* 'Wilsonii'

> The wonder tree produces large hanging clusters of pea-sized berries that turn deep red in autumn.

for its striking foliage and fruit, and makes a handsome shade tree. To obtain the fruit, both male and female plants are needed.

## Cultivation

Grow in sun or part-shade. Moderately fertile, moist but well-drained neutral to acid soil and a cool to warm-temperate climate are best. Prune when young to establish a single main trunk and a shapely crown. Propagate from seed in autumn or cuttings in summer.

### Idesia polycarpa

This fast-growing, shapely tree grows to a height of 40 ft (12 m), with a broad crown spreading to 20 ft (6 m). It has large heart-shaped, red-stalked dark green leaves; fragrant, greenish flowers are borne in spring and summer. *Idesia polycarpa* is frost hardy, particularly after long, hot summers which promote well-ripened wood. Female plants produce large hanging clusters of pea-sized berries that turn deep red in autumn. Zones 6–10.

## ILEX

*Holly*

The 400 or so evergreen and deciduous trees and shrubs that make up this large genus come mostly from the temperate regions of the northern hemisphere. They are grown for their foliage and clusters of small glossy berries. Hollies make excellent hedges, border plants, tub plants or screens for privacy. Male and female plants must be grown together to obtain the red, yellow or black berries in summer, autumn or winter. Clusters of small, greenish-white flowers precede them.

## Cultivation

Hollies grow well in deep, friable, well-drained soils with high organic content. They are fully to marginally frost hardy. An open, sunny position is best in cool climates. Water in hot, dry summers. Hollies do not like transplanting. Prune carefully in spring to check vigorous growth. Propagate from seed or cuttings. Check for signs of holly aphid and holly leaf miner.

### Ilex × altaclerensis

#### Highclere holly

This group of evergreen hybrid hollies, reaching a height of about 50 ft (15 m), has larger, variable leaves and larger flowers and berries than the English holly (*Ilex aquifolium*). Its many cultivars cover a range of plant sizes, fruit color and foliage variegations. Able to resist pollution and harsh coastal conditions, this is a useful plant for industrial and maritime areas. Zones 6–10.

### Ilex aquifolium

#### English holly

Native to Europe, North Africa and western Asia, this evergreen is a popular Christmas decoration in the northern hemisphere with its glossy, spiny-edged dark green leaves and bright red winter berries. It reaches 40 ft (12 m) with a spread of about 15 ft (4.5 m) or more and has an erect, branching habit. Commonly grown cultivars include many variegated forms, plants with yellow or red berries and some with interesting shaped foliage or smooth, spineless leaves. Zones 6–10.

## JACARANDA

This genus consists of about 50 species of medium to large deciduous and evergreen trees from Brazil and other parts of tropical and subtropical South America. All species have fern-like, bipinnate leaves and white, purple or mauve-blue, bell-shaped flowers. The best-known species, the mauve-blue *Jacaranda mimosifolia*, is one of the most widely planted and admired of all warm-climate

*Jacaranda mimosifolia*

*Juglans regia*

flowering trees. It yields a richly figured timber, although as the tree is so valued as an ornamental it is rarely cut.

## Cultivation
Marginally frost hardy, they grow in fertile, well-drained soil and full sun. Young plants need protection from frost. Potted specimens should be watered freely when in full growth, less so at other times. Propagate from seed in spring or from cuttings in summer.

### Jacaranda mimosifolia

**syns** *Jacaranda acutifolia*, *J. ovalifolia*
**Jacaranda**

From the high plains of Brazil, Paraguay and Argentina, this fast-growing, deciduous tree can reach 50 ft (15 m) in height with a spread of up to 40 ft (12 m). It has a broad, rounded crown. The vivid green, fern-like foliage is bipinnate, with 12 or more leaflets. Depending on climate, the leaves may be shed in winter or early spring before the flowers—mauve-blue to lilac terminal clusters of trumpet-shaped blossoms—appear; flat, leathery seed pods follow. Pruning is not desirable; if branches are removed, they are replaced by vertical shoots which spoil the shape of the tree. Zones 9–11.

## JUGLANS
Walnut

This genus, consisting of 15 species of deciduous trees, is distributed from the Mediterranean region and the Middle East to East Asia and North and South America. They are grown for their handsome form and elegant, aromatic foliage. All species bear edible nuts—usually produced within 12 years—and several yield fine timber used in furniture-making. Greenish-yellow male catkins and inconspicuous female flowers appear on the same tree in spring before the large pinnate leaves. They are followed by the hard-shelled nuts. The fallen leaves are said to be toxic to other plants (so do not put them on the compost heap). These are excellent ornamental trees for parks and large gardens.

## Cultivation
Cool-climate trees, they prefer a sunny position. Although quite frost hardy, young plants and the new spring growth are susceptible to frost damage. Deep rich alluvial soil of a light, loamy texture suits them best, and they need regular water. Propagate from freshly collected seed in autumn.

### Juglans regia

**Common walnut, Persian walnut, English walnut**

From southeastern Europe and temperate Asia, this slow-growing tree reaches 50 ft (15 m) tall with a spread of 30 ft (9 m). It has a sturdy trunk, a broad, leafy canopy and smooth, pale gray bark. The leaves are purplish-bronze when young, and yellow-green catkins appear from late spring to early summer. They are followed by the edible nut, enclosed in a green husk that withers and falls. The timber is valued for furniture-making. Cultivars include '**Wilson's Wonder**', which fruits younger than most at about 7 years old. Zones 4–10.

## JUNIPERUS
Juniper

Slow-growing and long-lived, the 50 or so species of evergreen shrubs and trees in this conifer genus occur throughout the northern hemisphere. Juvenile foliage is needle-like, but at maturity many species develop shorter scale-like leaves, closely pressed to the stem and exuding a pungent smell when crushed. Both types of foliage are found on adult trees of some species. Male and female cones usually occur on separate plants. The bluish-black or reddish seed

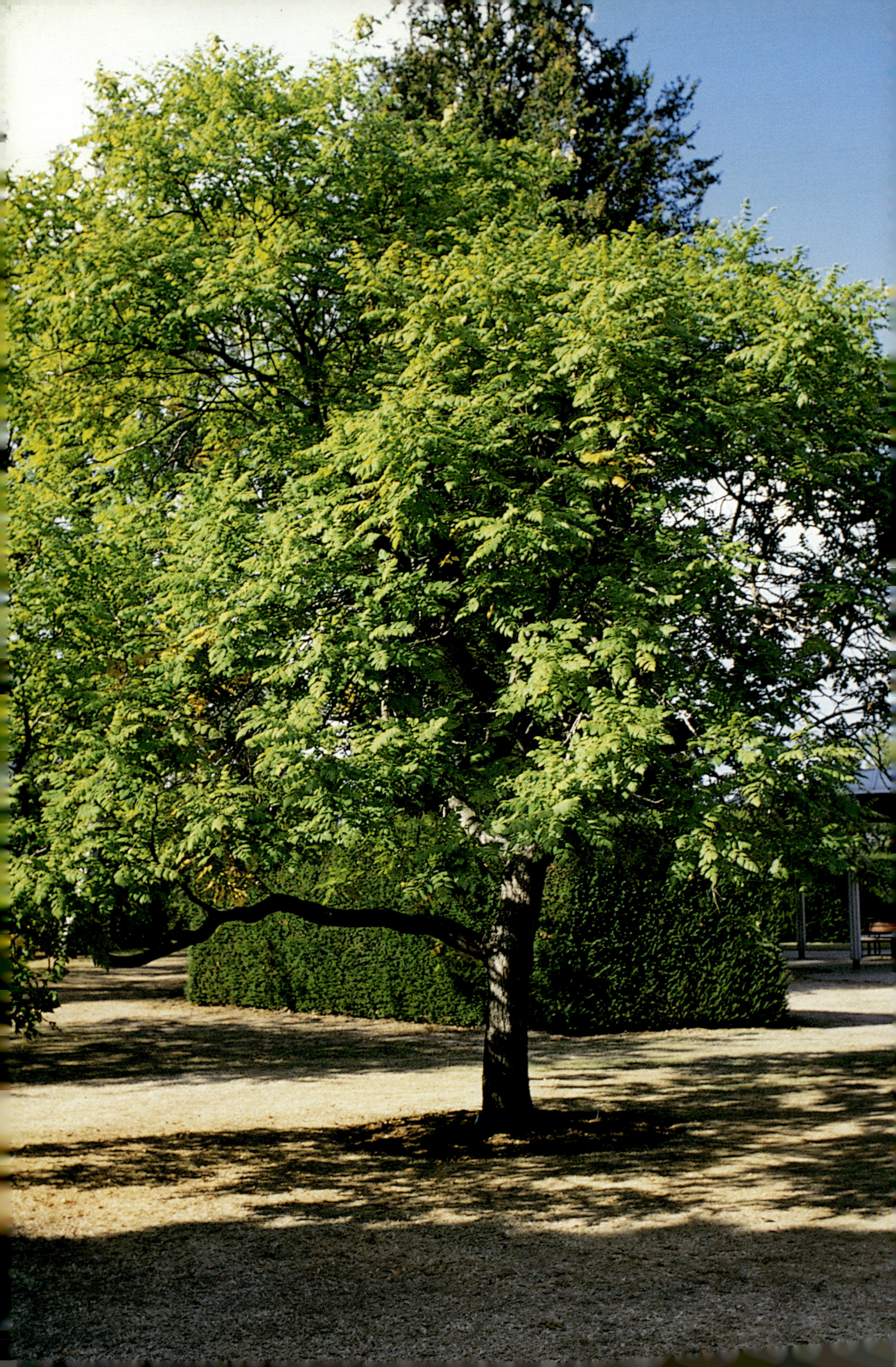

*niperus chinensis*　　　　　　　　　　*Koelreuteria paniculata*

cones have fleshy, fused scales; known as berries, some of which are used to flavor gin. The fragrant, pinkish, cedar-like timber is soft but durable. Various species of juniper are used medicinally.

## Cultivation

Easily cultivated in a cool climate, they prefer a sunny position and any well-drained soil. Prune to maintain shape or restrict size, but do not make visible cuts as old, leafless wood rarely sprouts. Propagate from cuttings in winter, layers if low-growing, or from seed; cultivars can be propagated by grafting.

### Juniperus chinensis

**Chinese juniper**

Native to the Himalayas, China, Mongolia and Japan, this frost-hardy species usually matures to a conical tree up to 50 ft (15 m) in height with a spread of 6–10 ft (1.8–3 m). Sometimes, however, it forms a low-spreading shrub. Both adult and juvenile foliage may be found on adult trees. The berries are fleshy and glaucous white. '**Aurea**' grows to at least 35 ft (11 m) tall, with a conical habit and soft, golden foliage; '**Kaizuka**' is a small tree to 20 ft (6 m), with twisted spear-like branches; '**Pyramidalis**' grows to 15 ft (4.5 m) tall, with dense, blue-green leaves and a columnar habit; and '**Variegata**' grows to 20 ft (6 m) tall, glaucous with white markings. Zones 4–9.

### Juniperus virginiana

**Eastern red cedar, Pencil cedar**

From North America, this is the tallest of the junipers commonly grown in gardens, reaching 50–60 ft (15–18 m) in height. It has a conical or broadly columnar habit and both scale- and needle-like gray-green leaves. The berries are fleshy, small, glaucous and brownish-violet. The wood is used in making lead pencils, hence the common name.

'**Glauca**', a columnar form with blue-green foliage, grows to 25 ft (8 m) tall with a spread of 8 ft (2.4 m). Zones 2–9.

## Koelreuteria

Grown for their foliage, flowers and decorative fruit, this small genus of 3 species of deciduous trees is from dry valley woodland in East Asia. They are useful small trees with pyramid-shaped panicles of long, bowl-shaped flowers followed by inflated fruit capsules.

## Cultivation

Moderately frost hardy, they thrive in full sun in fertile, well-aerated soil with free drainage. They can withstand hot, dry summers, but seaside conditions do not suit them. Propagate from root cuttings in late winter or from seed in autumn. Prune in the early years to establish a single trunk.

### Koelreuteria paniculata

**Golden rain tree, Varnish tree**

From China and Korea, this slow-growing, wide-spreading tree can reach 30–50 ft (9–15 m), but is often smaller in gardens. It has a convex crown and a single or divided main trunk. The bark is furrowed and the branches droop at the ends. The mid-green leaflets turn deep golden yellow to orange in autumn. Large clusters of clear yellow flowers are borne in summer and are followed by papery, bladder-like, pinkish-brown pods. It does well in alkaline soil. '**September**' (syn. '**September Gold**') is similar to the species, except that it flowers late in the season. Zones 4–10.

## Laburnum

*Golden chain tree*

Two species of deciduous small trees from Europe and western Asia make up this genus of legumes,

Opposite: *Koelreuteria paniculata*

*Laburnum × watereri* 'Vossi'

*Lagerstroemia indica*

## 56

### TREES

allied to *Cytisus* and other brooms. They have compound leaves with 3 leaflets that are larger and thinner than other members of the broom tribe, and the bright yellow pea-flowers borne in profuse pendulous sprays are also relatively large; they are followed by brown seed pods. All parts of the tree are very poisonous; handle with gloves.

## Cultivation

Cool-climate plants, they prefer full sun, some humidity and tolerate any moderately fertile soil with free drainage—they do not like being waterlogged. Prune competing leaders in the early years to establish a tree-like form. Owners of large gardens may create 'laburnum arches' of 2 rows of trees tied down over a trellis, so that the flower sprays hang below like wisterias. Watch for leaf miner insects; protect young trees from snails. Propagate species from seed in autumn, cultivars by budding in summer.

### *Laburnum × watereri*

**Voss laburnum, Waterer laburnum**

Now the most commonly grown laburnum, this hybrid between *Laburnum anagyroides* and *L. alpinum* makes a tree of similar size to the parent species. It has dark green leaflets and in late spring and early summer it produces dense racemes up to 18 in (45 cm) in length of fragrant rich yellow flowers.

'**Vossii**', the cultivar most commonly seen in nurseries, produces rich, buttercup yellow flowers on 24 in (60 cm) long racemes. Zones 3–9.

## LAGERSTROEMIA

*Crape (or crepe) myrtle*

From southern and eastern Asia and ranging as far as northern Australia, this is a genus of around 50 species of evergreen and deciduous small to large trees, a few grown in warm and hot climates for their showy flowers. Their most distinctive feature is the crinkly margin and slender basal stalk of each of the 5 petals that make up a flower; the flowers in turn are massed into large, dense panicles at the branch tips. The 'crape' (alternatively crepe) in the name arose from the flowers' texture being reminiscent of the once-popular fabric crape, while 'myrtle' alludes to their being close relatives to the large myrtle family. They make fine garden plants and are easily grown. Some species have attractive smooth, green, brown or reddish bark. The timber of some species is highly prized for shipbuilding.

## Cultivation

These plants thrive in full sun in well-drained, humus-rich soil. Shelter from strong summer winds, which destroy the delicate flowers. Propagate from cuttings in summer or from seed in spring. Watch for powdery mildew.

### *Lagerstroemia indica*

**Crape (or crepe) myrtle, Pride of India**

This deciduous tree grows to about 25 ft (8 m) tall with an open, spreading, rounded head and smooth beige bark streaked red-brown. In mid- to late summer it bears large clusters of frilly pink to deep red flowers. In cool areas, the small oval leaves turn gold in autumn. Flowerheads are largest on strong growths, encouraged by pruning the main branches in winter; if not pruned, the tree develops an attractive, open shape, with massed smaller heads. The typical form of this species is now almost forgotten in cultivation, replaced by an array of cultivars, including some of dwarf habit. Zones 6–11.

## LARIX

*Larch*

From cool mountainous regions of the northern hemisphere, these deciduous, fast-growing conifers

*Laburnum × watereri* 'Vossii'

*The common laurel has been grown as an ornamental since ancient times and has always had great symbolic significance.*

*Larix decidua*

*Laurus nobilis*

have a handsome, graceful form and fresh green spring foliage as well as strong, durable timber; the bark also is used for tanning and dyeing. Mainly conical in shape, they lose their leaves in autumn, bursting into leaf in early spring. With the new foliage appear both drooping yellow male (pollen) cones and upright red female cones, which mature over the following summer to short, erect seed cones with thin scales; these persist on the tree after shedding their seeds. Up to 15 species of *Larix* have been recognized, but recent studies have merged some of these, reducing this number to as few as 9 species.

## Cultivation
Cold- to cool-climate plants, they do best in well-drained, light or gravelly soil; most resent waterlogged soil. Propagation is from seed. Check regularly for larch canker or blister and infestation by larch chermes (a type of aphid).

### Larix decidua

**European larch**

From the mountains of central and southern Europe, this tree reaches a height of 100 ft (30 m); it has a conical crown when young, spreading with maturity. The branches are widely spaced and the branchlets have a graceful, weeping habit. The soft, bright green, needle-like leaves turn yellow in autumn before dropping. The mature seed cones are egg-shaped, brown and upright. The gray bark becomes red-brown, fissured and scaly with age. Zones 2–9.

## LAURUS

This genus consists of 2 species of evergreen shrubs and trees from the Mediterranean region, Canary Islands and the Azores. The common laurel (*Laurus nobilis*) has been grown as an ornamental since ancient times and has always had great symbolic significance. Among other uses, its dark green leaves have been used in funeral and remembrance wreaths, though the glossy leaves of the unrelated cherry laurel (*Prunus laurocerasus*) are now generally substituted. The highly aromatic leaves are also dried and used as a culinary herb (an essential ingredient in bouquet garni). Both species are useful evergreen screen plants and tub specimens, and are often used for topiary.

## Cultivation
Cool- to warm-climate plants, they are moderately frost hardy and do best in sheltered positions in sun or part-shade in fertile, well-drained soil. They are tolerant of coastal conditions. Propagation is from seed in autumn or from cuttings in summer.

### Laurus nobilis

**Sweet bay, Bay tree, Bay laurel, Laurel**

A broadly conical tree, this species grows up to 40 ft (12 m) high and 30 ft (9 m) wide, but is generally smaller in cultivation. Its glossy, dark green leaves are smooth and leathery and in classical times were used to make the victor's 'crown of laurels'. It produces small, star-shaped, fragrant yellowish flowers in late spring to early summer, followed by small, round, green berries that ripen to dark purplish-black in autumn. This tree is suited to clipping and shaping. '**Aurea**' is a yellow-leafed form and '**Saratoga**' is best suited to training as a single-trunked tree. Zones 7–10.

## LIQUIDAMBAR

This is a genus of 4 species of deciduous trees from Turkey, East Asia, North America and Mexico belonging to the witch-hazel family, grown for their shapely form, handsome foliage and superb autumn colors. The leaves are deeply lobed, resembling a typical maple leaf. Some species produce a resinous gum known as liquid storax

*Liquidambar styraciflua*

*Liriodendron tulipifera*

> The tulip tree's distinctive leaves look as though someone has cut their ends off with scissors.

that is used to scent soap, as an expectorant in cough remedies and in the treatment of some skin diseases.

## Cultivation

They are temperate-climate plants, requiring sun or part-shade and fertile, deep, loamy soil with adequate water during spring and summer. They will not thrive in shallow, sandy soil. The trees are best allowed to develop their lower branches to ground level. Propagate by budding in spring or from seed in autumn.

### *Liquidambar styraciflua*

**Sweet gum**

This widely grown deciduous tree is native to eastern USA and Mexico and reaches a height of 80 ft (24 m) and spread of 40 ft (12 m). Young branches and twigs often have distinctive ridges of corky bark and its wood, known commercially as satin walnut, is used for furniture-making. It bears glossy dark green leaves that color orange to red and purple in autumn. Globular heads of small yellow-green flowers appear in spring, followed by spiky, ball-like fruit clusters. Some cultivars valued for their rich autumn coloring include '**Moraine**'; '**Burgundy**': deep purple-red; '**Festival**': pink through yellow; '**Palo Alto**': orange-red; '**Rotundiloba**', an odd form with the leaves having very rounded lobes; '**Variegata**': streaked yellow; and '**Worplesdon**': purple through orange-yellow. Zones 5–11.

## LIRIODENDRON

*Tulip tree*

Some botanists recognize only *Liriodendron tulipifera* in this genus. Most, however, accept *L. chinense* as a species also, not just as a variety. Their 4-lobed leaves are distinctive: they look as though someone has cut their ends off with scissors. The flowers are distinctive too, in pale green with orange at the bases and numerous stamens. They do not, in fact, look much like tulips, but are more like their cousins the magnolias. Both are handsome trees, with straight boles and symmetrical crowns, though they are too big and fast-growing for any but the largest of gardens.

## Cultivation

They prefer a temperate climate, sun or part-shade and deep, fertile, well-drained, slightly acid soil. Propagate from seed or by grafting. They are difficult to transplant.

### *Liriodendron tulipifera*

From eastern USA, this is an outstanding tree for cool climates, reaching 100 ft (30 m) or more with a spread of about 50 ft (15 m). A vigorous grower with a broadly conical habit, it bears deep green, lobed leaves that turn rich golden yellow in autumn. Its summer-blooming flowers are followed by conical brown fruit. The pale timber, called 'yellow poplar', is not very hard or durable but is fairly light and strong and much used in furniture-making. '**Aureomarginatum**' has green leaves heavily edged with yellow; '**Fastigiatum**' is about half the size, with an erect, columnar form. Zones 4–10.

## MAGNOLIA

This large, varied genus of 100 or more species of deciduous and evergreen trees and shrubs from East Asia and the Americas was named after French botanist Pierre Magnol. Magnolia leaves are usually oval and smooth-edged. The flowers are generally large, fragrant and solitary, come in white, yellow, pink or purple, and vary in shape from almost flat and saucer-like to a narrow goblet shape. The fruits are cone-like or roughly cylindrical.

Magnolia campbellii

Magnolia grandiflora

## Cultivation

Magnolias require deep, fertile, well-drained soil. Some species require alkaline soil while others prefer a mildly acid, humus-rich soil. The roots are fragile so the plants do not transplant readily. They thrive in sun or part-shade but need protection from strong or salty winds. The flower buds are frost sensitive. Propagate from cuttings in summer or seed in autumn, or by grafting in winter.

### Magnolia campbellii

This deciduous Himalayan species grows 80 ft (24 m) tall with a 40 ft (12 m) wide crown. Slightly fragrant flowers appear on leafless branches from late winter to mid-spring. Plants raised from seed take 20 or more years to flower. '**Alba**' has pure white flowers; '**Charles Raffill**' is white and rose purple; '**Lanarth**' is a deeper rose-purple; and *Magnolia campbellii* subsp. *mollicomata* flowers at an earlier age. Zones 7–10.

### Magnolia grandiflora

**Southern magnolia, Bull bay**

One of the few cultivated evergreen magnolias, this southern USA species forms a dense 60–80 ft (18–24 m) dome of deep green leathery leaves, rust-colored underneath. Cup-shaped white or cream blooms 10 in (25 cm) across appear during late summer, followed by reddish-brown cones. It usually prefers warm, moist conditions, but many cultivars (including the Freeman hybrids with *Magnolia virginiana*) are hardier; others, such as '**Exmouth**', have a more conical habit and fragrant flowers from an early age. '**Edith Bogue**' is renowned for its cold tolerance. Narrow semi-dwarf '**Little Gem**', with smaller flowers, reaches up to 12 ft (3.5 m) tall or so in 15 years. '**Russett**' has a compact upright habit with beige suede-like leaf undersides and comparatively large flowers to 12 in (30 cm) across. Zones 6–11.

### Magnolia × soulangeana

**Saucer magnolia**

This deciduous hybrid between *Magnolia denudata* and *M. liliiflora* first appeared in Europe in the 1820s. An erect tree to 25 ft (8 m) tall and 15 ft (4.5 m) wide, it is usually single-trunked. The dark green leaves are tapered at the base and rounded at the tip, with a short point. Blooms in goblet, cup or saucer shapes and in white, pink or deep purple-pink appear from late winter to mid-spring, before and after the leaves emerge. '**Alexandrina**' flowers are pure white inside, flushed rose-purple outside; and '**Brozzonii**' has large white flowers, purple at the base. Goblet-shaped cultivars include '**Lennei**', purplish-pink outside, white to pale purple inside; '**Lennei Alba**' with pure white flowers; and '**Rustica Rubra**', rose-red outside and pink and white inside. Zones 5–10.

## MALUS

*Apple, crabapple*

This genus of 35 species of deciduous flowering and fruiting trees from the northern temperate zones contains the diverse crabapple as well as the many varieties of the long-cultivated edible apple, probably derived from crosses between several species and usually named *Malus × domestica* or *M. pumila*. The leaves are simple and toothed, sometimes lobed, and the flower clusters vary from white to deep rose-pink or deep reddish-purple. They are valued for their shapely form, moderate size and delicate spring blossom.

### Cultivation

Very frost hardy, they prefer a cool, moist climate and full sun (but tolerate part-shade) and need fertile, well-drained, loamy soil with protection from strong winds. They grow in poorer soils if fertilized annually. Cut out dead wood in winter and prune for a balanced shape. Propagate by

**TREES**

*Malus floribunda*     *Malus × purpurea*     *Melaleuca quinquenervia*

budding in summer or grafting in winter. Watch for aphids and fireblight.

### Malus floribunda

**Japanese crab**

This parent of many hybrids grows 25 ft (8 m) tall with a broad 30 ft (9 m) crown and arching branches. It bears profuse, pale pink flowers, red in bud, and tiny, pea-shaped, yellowish-blushed red fruit. It is thought to have been introduced to Japan from China. Zones 4–9.

### Malus, ornamental crabapples

This group includes '**Beverly**', an upright spreading tree to 20 ft (6 m) high with white single flowers and small bright red fruit; '**Butterball**', up to 25 ft (8 m) tall with pink-tinged white flowers and bright orange-yellow fruit; '**Candied Apple**', a small, spreading tree with pink flowers and red fruit; '**Dolgo**', to 40 ft (12 m) with white flowers and purple-red fruit; '**John Downie**', conical when mature, with red-flushed orange fruit; '**Katherine**' with semi-double pink flowers and rich red fruit blushed yellow; '**Pink Perfection**' with pale pink and white double flowers; '**Prince Georges**' with sterile, scented fully double pale pink flowers; '**Profusion**' with rich, dark wine-red flowers and cherry-like, red-purple fruit; and '**Radiant**', to 25 ft (8 m) high with deep red buds, deep pink single flowers and bright red fruit. Zones 3–9.

### Malus × purpurea

These hybrid trees have very dark, sometimes glossy, bark and bronze or purple-red foliage. The flowers are large, red to purple-red, followed by small fruit of a similar color. Cultivars include '**Aldenhamensis**', a spreading tree to 25 ft (8 m) with semi-double, wine-red flowers and purple-red fruit; and '**Eleyi**' with purple leaves, deep crimson flowers and purple-red fruit. Zones 4–9.

## MELALEUCA
*Paperbark*

The evergreen trees and shrubs that form this large genus are indigenous to Australia, except for a few species from Papua New Guinea, Indonesia and coastal Southeast Asia. Some species have beautiful papery bark which peels off in large sheets. They bear profuse, brush-like flowers with showy stamens, and their nectar provides food for birds and small mammals. The leathery leaves are small and cylindrical or flat.

### Cultivation

Adaptable plants, they tolerate wet, even boggy conditions (but prefer well-drained soil), pollution, and salt-laden winds and soil. Although warm-climate plants, most species withstand light frosts if in full sun. Propagate from seed or cuttings taken just as growth begins. Prune shrubby species lightly straight after flowering. Melaleucas are remarkably pest- and disease-free.

### Melaleuca armillaris

**Bracelet honey myrtle, Drooping melaleuca**

This 30 ft (9 m) tree has a spreading canopy of deep green needle-like leaves. The buds are usually pink or red, opening to white flowers in cylindrical spikes up to 2 in (5 cm) long in spring and summer. The gray, furrowed bark peels off in strips. Fast-growing, it adapts to a wide range of soil types. Zones 9–11.

### Melaleuca quinquenervia

**Broad-leafed paperbark, Punk tree**

Best known of the broad-leaved melaleucas, this is a popular street and park tree in warm climates; it

**Opposite:** *Melaleuca armillaris*

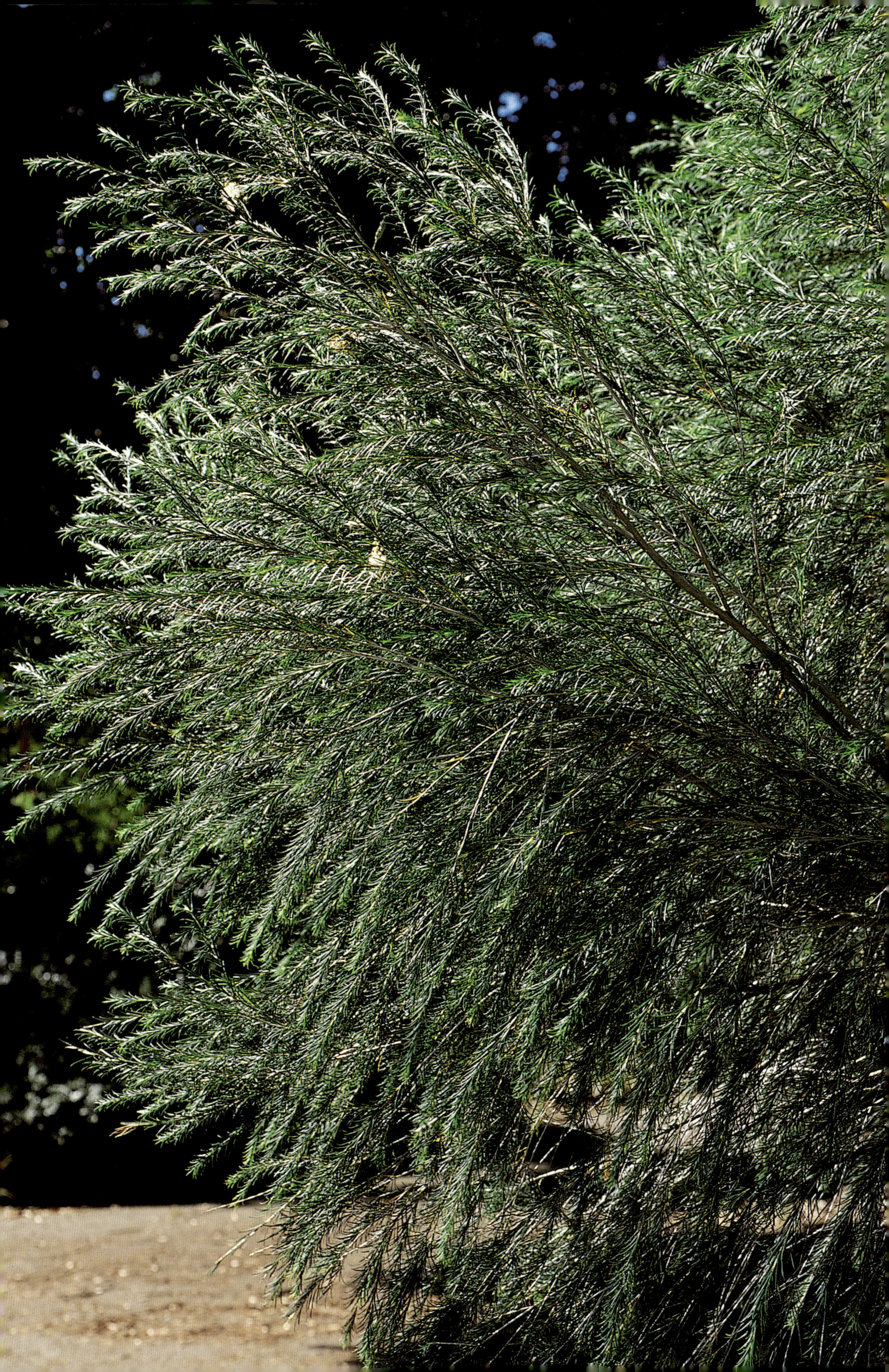

*Melia azedarach*  *Melia azedarach (detail)*  *Metasequoia glyptostroboides*

has become thoroughly naturalized in the Florida Everglades to the concern of environmentalists. Native to east-coastal Australia and New Caledonia, it usually grows in swamps, but adapts to quite dry soil in cultivation. The cream bark is very thick and papery, the leaves stiff and flat, and the white flowers appear in spring and sporadically at other times. It grows to 60 ft (18 m) or more tall. Zones 10–12.

## Melia
*Persian lilac, White cedar, Chinaberry, Bead tree, Rosary tree*

This genus of only one very variable species of deciduous tree ranges across Asia from Iraq to Japan and south to Australia. *Melia azedarach* has many common names; 2 of them, bead tree and rosary tree, arise from the way the seeds have a hole through the middle, convenient for bead-making. The trees were formerly grown in southern Italy for making rosaries. *Melia* is Greek for 'ash' (*Fraxinus*), although the only connection is that the pinnate or doubly pinnate leaves are vaguely similar.

### Cultivation
A warm-climate plant, tolerating dry conditions and poor soil, it is a favorite street tree in arid climates. Propagate from seed in autumn.

### *Melia azedarach*

syn. ***Melia azedarach* var. *australasica***

This is a fast-growing, spreading tree which grows to 30 ft (9 m) tall. The young leaves appear in late spring or early summer, with large sprays of small, delicately scented lilac flowers; these are followed by bunches of pale orange or cream berries, each containing a single woody seed, which persist after the leaves fall. They are poisonous to humans but much eaten by birds. '**Umbraculiformis**' has a curious yet attractive habit, like a blown-out umbrella. Zones 8–12.

## Metasequoia
*Dawn redwood*

Until shortly after World War II, *Metasequoia glyptostroboides*, the single species of the genus, was known only as a fossil conifer. Then a stand of living trees was discovered in western China; from these it has been propagated and widely planted in temperate-climate areas. It is notable for its gold and russet foliage in autumn—it is one of the few deciduous conifers. It grows very rapidly and, as the timber is durable and of fine quality, it is a very promising tree for cool-climate forestry.

### Cultivation
It prefers full sun, deep fertile soil, good summer rainfall and shelter from strong winds. It is fully frost hardy. Propagate from seed or cuttings from side shoots in autumn.

### *Metasequoia glyptostroboides*

Its gracefully conical outline and delicate foliage, light green in spring and summer, have made the dawn redwood a popular tree. It grows unusually fast in favorable conditions, and old trees may reach 200 ft (60 m) in height. As the tree matures, the rough-textured bark turns from reddish to dark brown to gray. It can be clipped to make a tall hedge. Zones 5–10.

## Metrosideros

The 50 or so species in this South Pacific genus are not all trees; some are shrubs or clinging vines. They are especially important in New Zealand where several species yield rata—the hard, dark red timber prized by the Maori for

*Metrosideros umbellatus*

*Michelia doltsopa*

carving—and where they range from the very edge of the sea to the high mountains. They have hard, leathery, evergreen leaves, often gray tinged, and red (sometimes bright yellow) summer flowers whose chief beauty, like those of the related *Eucalyptus* of Australia, comes from their long colored stamens.

## Cultivation

Moderately frost hardy to frost tender, they do best in subtropical or warm-temperate climates, in full sun or light shade and fertile, well-drained soil. The shrubby species do very well as container plants. Propagate from seed in spring or cuttings in summer.

### Metrosideros excelsus

**syn. *Metrosideros tomentosus***
**Pohutukawa, New Zealand Christmas tree**

Reaching 40 ft (12 m) in height, this tree begins as a shrub with dense masses of spreading branches, then develops a stout main trunk and umbrella-shaped canopy. The oblong leaves are glossy deep green above—and gray and felty underneath. The crimson stamens stand out from the flowers, borne from late spring to mid-summer in warm zones. The pohutukawa will survive in the most exposed seashore situations, as long as the soil is not saline. '**Variegata**', with creamy yellow-edged leaves, is a popular cultivar. Zones 10–11.

### Metrosideros umbellatus

**Southern rata**

Similar to the northern rata, although not as large, this species occurs almost throughout New Zealand and extends into higher alpine regions. It produces masses of intensely scarlet blooms from late spring to autumn and its flowering is a feature of the bushlands of the Southern Alps. It grows very slowly. Zones 8–10.

## MICHELIA

Closely related to the magnolias, the 45 or so species of *Michelia* are found in tropical and subtropical Asia, with a few species in the cooler foothills of the Himalayas. They range from shrubs to substantial trees, mainly evergreen, and many bear intensely fragrant flowers. Some species are widely cultivated in India for their fragrant oil, which is extracted from the blooms for use in perfume and cosmetics.

## Cultivation

They like frost-free climates and a position in full sun or part-shade in humus-rich, well-drained, neutral to acid soil; they resent being transplanted. Propagate from seed in autumn or spring, or from cuttings in summer.

### Michelia doltsopa

This 30 ft (9 m) tree from the eastern Himalayas is slender while young, developing a broader crown with age. The large, scented white flowers, resembling those of *Magnolia denudata*, appear in the axils of the glossy green leaves in late winter and early spring. '**Silver Cloud**' was selected due to its incredibly abundant flower production; otherwise it is identical to the species. Zones 9–11.

## MORUS
*Mulberry*

There are about 10 species of deciduous shrubs and trees in this northern hemisphere genus. They bear broad, roughly heart shaped leaves with closely toothed margins; the leaves on seedlings may be deeply lobed. Catkins of inconspicuous greenish flowers develop into tiny fruits, closely packed together to appear as a single fruit, the mulberry. Some species have been cultivated for centuries, for their edible fruit and for silk production: the silkworm larvae feed on the leaves.

TREES

*Morus alba* — *Nothofagus cunninghamii*

## Cultivation

They thrive under a wide range of conditions, but do best in fertile, well-drained soil in a sunny, sheltered position. Propagate from cuttings in winter, which can be quite large branches.

### Morus alba

**syn. *Morus bombycis***
**White mulberry, Silkworm mulberry**

This vigorous, low-branching tree has sustained the silk industry of China and Japan. It grows up to 40 ft (12 m) tall, with a broadly spreading crown and pendulous smaller branches. The almost hairless leaves are a fresh green-yellow in autumn, strongly veined and with sharp teeth. The rather rubbery fruit are cylindrical, sometimes lanceolate, and color varies from white through pink or red to purple-black. In east-coastal Australia a strain with purple-black fruit is regarded as the common mulberry. It prefers a climate with long, warm summers. '**Pendula**' is a mushroom-shaped weeping form usually grafted onto standards to give initial height. Zones 5–10.

## NOTHOFAGUS
*southern beech*

Wide ranging in the southern hemisphere from South America to southeastern Australia, *Nothofagus* is a genus that contains more than 25 species of evergreen and deciduous trees. They are fast-growing, and have dark green leaves often with toothed margins. The foliage of several of the deciduous species displays rich bronze hues before dropping in autumn. The small fruits each contain 3 triangular seeds, which are commonly known as beechnuts.

## Cultivation

Southern beeches can be cultivated in a variety of climates provided they have protection from strong winds. They prefer acid soil deep enough to support their large root system and should be planted out when small and never transplanted. Position in full sun and water well when young. Propagate from cuttings in summer or seed in autumn.

### Nothofagus cunninghamii

**Tasmanian beech, Myrtle beech**

This magnificent tree attains a height of 150 ft (45 m) or more when grown in the cool, mountainous regions of its native southern Australia. An evergreen, it is one of the faster-growing species in the genus, and is valued for its reddish timber. Its small, triangular-toothed leaves are held in fan-shaped sprays and the young foliage is a deep bronze shade in spring. Small catkin flowers are borne in early summer. Zones 8–9.

### Nothofagus menziesii

**New Zealand silver beech**

Famed for its beautiful silver bark, this evergreen species from New Zealand bears a mass of small, dense leaves with coarsely serrated margins. Reaching a height of 70 ft (21 m), it needs plenty of sun and protection from wind. The flowers appear as small catkins in summer. Zones 7–10.

## NYSSA
*Tupelo*

Occurring naturally in southern Asia and North America, this genus is named after Nyssa, the water nymph, because the trees insist on adequate year-round water to survive. Fast-growing and wind tolerant, they must be left undisturbed after planting and may reach a maximum height of 120 ft (36 m) with a broad-based, conical shape. Small clusters of greenish-white flowers appear during summer, followed by vivid, dark purple berries up to 1 in (25 mm) long which provide an effective

*Nyssa sylvatica*

*Olea europaea* subsp. *europaea*

contrast to the stunning foliage. Few trees attract as much attention when they are clad in their spectacular red, crimson, yellow and orange autumn foliage.

## Cultivation

They need fertile, moist but well-drained, neutral to acid soil, sun or part-shade and a cool climate. Prune only to remove dead or crowded branches. Propagate from cuttings in summer or from seed in autumn.

### Nyssa sylvatica

**Black tupelo, Sour gum, Pepperidge**

This elegant tree is one of the most decorative and useful of all deciduous plants, as it flourishes in swampy conditions. The glossy 4 in (10 cm) long leaves, which are slightly wider toward the tip, are dark or yellowish-green then turn brilliant red, often with shades of orange and yellow as well, before dropping. It grows to 70 ft (21 m) with a broad columnar conical habit and has an unusual trunk with brownish-gray bark that breaks up into large pieces on mature specimens. Zones 3–10.

## OLEA
*Olive*

There are about 20 species in this genus, all long-lived evergreen trees. They have leathery, narrow to broad leaves and tiny, off-white flowers that are followed by the fruit, known botanically as drupes. The most important species is the common olive (*Olea europaea*), which has many cultivars and is the source of olive oil. Since ancient times it has been cultivated around the Mediterranean for its nourishing, oil-rich fruit. The fruit is too bitter to be eaten fresh: it must be treated with lye (sodium hydroxide) before being pickled or preserved in its own oil. The wood of the olive tree is prized for carving and turning.

## Cultivation

Generally, these trees require a mild climate, but the winters need to be sufficiently cool to induce flowering, while the summers must be long and hot to ensure development and growth of the fruits. Although olives can survive on poor soils, better cropping will result if the trees are given a well-drained, fertile loam with ample moisture when the fruit is forming. Propagate from seed in autumn, from heel cuttings in winter or from suckers.

### Olea europaea

**Common olive**

*Olea europaea* is a tree of wide distribution in Africa, Arabia and Himalayan Asia. The cultivated olive, *O. e.* **subsp.** *europaea*, is believed to have derived from smaller-fruited plants thousands of years ago. A slow grower to about 30 ft (9 m), it is very long-lived, to compensate for its not coming into full bearing until it is at least 10 years old. Its picturesque habit, rough, gray bark and gray-green leaves, touched with silver on their undersides, make it a beautiful sight. *O. e.* **subsp.** *africana* has pea-sized black fruit and glossy dark green leaves, brown on the undersides. It makes a handsome small shade tree with a thick, gnarled trunk, but seeds itself so profusely as to become a problem weed in subtropical climates. Zones 8–11.

## OXYDENDRUM
*Sorrel tree, Sourwood*

The single deciduous tree species in this genus is a native of eastern USA and is grown for its autumn foliage and flowers. The leaves are alternate and finely toothed; the fragrant, small urn-shaped flowers are held in drooping terminal panicles. The genus takes its name from Greek words meaning 'sour tree', a reference to the sour-tasting foliage.

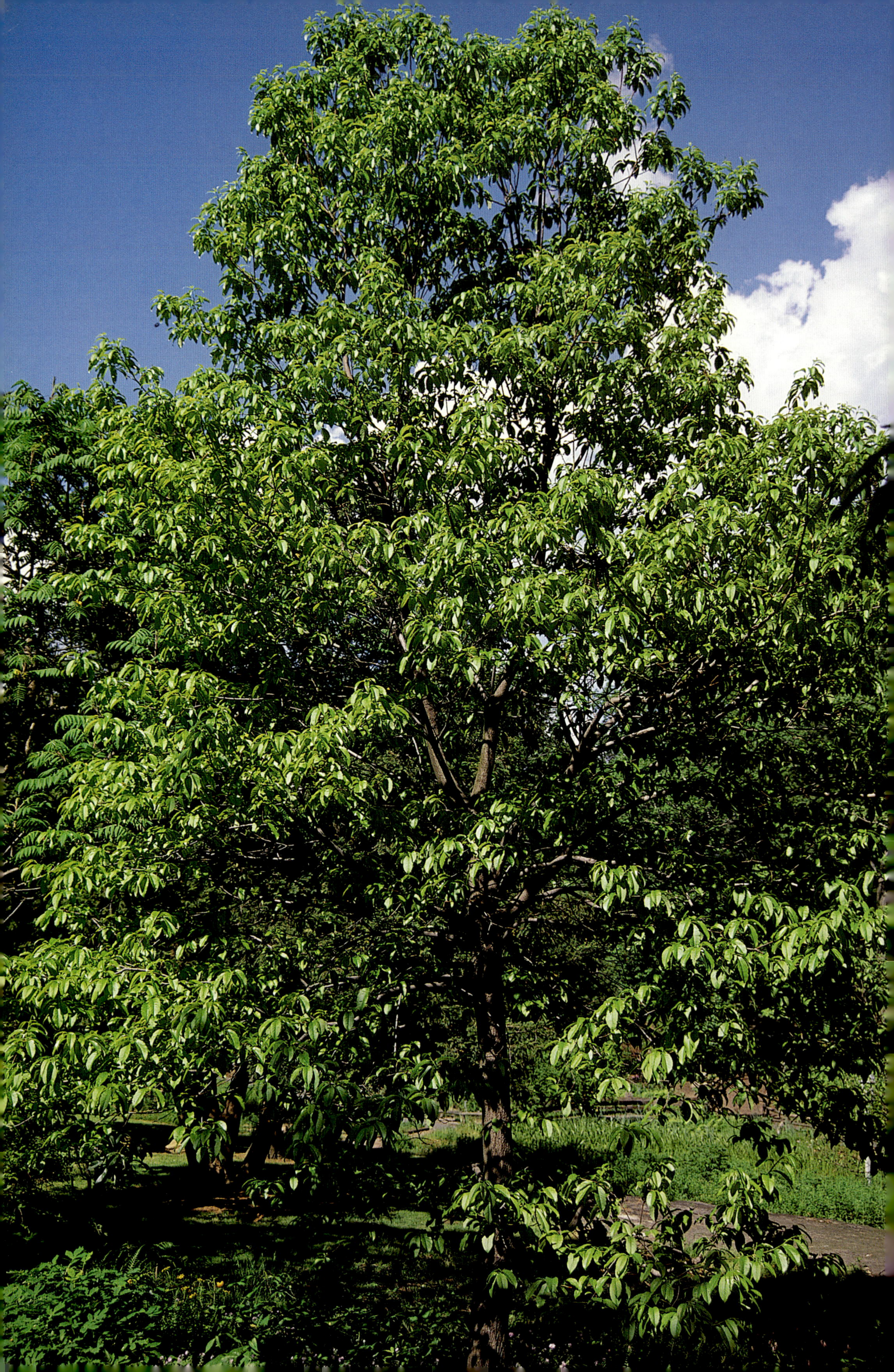

*Parrotia persica*

*Paulownia tomentosa*

## Cultivation

For the best autumn colors, it should be planted in an open position in sun or part-shade in moist soil. An occasional dressing of iron and/or ammonia after flowering may be required. Propagate from cuttings in summer or seed in autumn.

### Oxydendrum arboreum

A small, 20–40 ft (6–12 m) tree, this cool-climate species tolerates frost better than it does dry conditions. The trunk is slender and the crown pyramid-shaped. Streamers of small white lily-of-the-valley-like flowers appear in late summer sometimes prior to, sometimes coinciding with, the display of deep scarlet foliage. Zones 3–9.

## PARROTIA
*Persian witch-hazel*

This genus from Iran and the Caucasus was named after F. W. Parrot, a German botanist. It consists of one tree species grown for its rich autumn hues and unusual flowers. The petal-less flowers consist of upright, wiry, dark red stamens enclosed in brown bracts. They appear in early spring before the leaves, which are about 4 in (10 cm) long with undulating edges. The branches on older trees dip downward.

## Cultivation

A lime-tolerant tree, it is said to achieve its best colors when grown in slightly acid soil. It grows well in full sun, fertile soil and temperate climates. Propagate from softwood cuttings in summer or from seed in autumn—germination can take up to 18 months.

### Parrotia persica

This spreading, short-trunked, deciduous tree with flaking bark can reach 40 ft (12 m) in the wild, but rarely grows above 25 ft (8 m). The roughly diamond-shaped leaves turn magnificent shades of yellow, orange and crimson in autumn. Zones 5–9.

## PAULOWNIA

Originating in eastern Asia, some of the 17 species of deciduous trees in this genus grow very fast, to 8 ft (2.4 m) in their first year, eventually growing to 50 ft (15 m). Their big, heart-shaped leaves and dense clusters of elegant flowers make them distinctive shade trees. Conspicuous, attractive buds appear in autumn, opening in spring to foxglove-like flower spikes; leaves and wing-seeded capsules follow. Some species are grown for timber in China and Japan.

## Cultivation

Frost-hardy, they like well-drained, fertile soil, with ample moisture in summer and shelter from strong winds. Propagate from seed or root cuttings in late summer or winter.

### Paulownia tomentosa

syn. *Paulownia imperialis*
Princess tree, Empress tree

This tree, up to 40 ft (12 m) high and wide, is valued for its large, paired, heart-shaped leaves, up to 12 in (30 cm) wide, and erect, fragrant, pale violet flowers. Grown in both cool- and warm-temperate climates, it can suffer frost damage to the flower buds. If pruned almost to the ground each winter, the tree will develop branches about 10 ft (3 m) long with enormous leaves, but will not flower. Zones 5–10.

## PHELLODENDRON

Elegant, slender and requiring little maintenance, these 10 species of deciduous trees from East Asia grow to 50 ft (15 m) tall with a crown spreading to 12 ft (3.5 m). The shiny, light green pinnate leaves turn a rich shade of yellow in autumn. Small, yellowish-green flowers appear in

Opposite: *Oxydendron arboreum*

*Phellodendron amurense*

*Picea pungens*

late spring or early summer, followed by blackberry-like fruits.

## Cultivation

These trees are extremely hardy, tolerating both frost and harsh sun, although they prefer protection from wind. They grow best in full sun with fertile, well-drained soil. Seed may be germinated in spring, or propagate from cuttings or by grafting or layering in summer.

### Phellodendron amurense

**Amur cork tree**

Originally from China and Japan, this is the most common species of the genus in cultivation and earns its common name from its corky older branches. Growing to 40 ft (12 m) tall, it prefers humus-rich soil and summer moisture. Its bright green leaves with 5 to 11 leaflets have an unusual heart-shaped base and a pungent aroma. The 5-petalled flowers, male and female on separate trees, produce berries that are held above the foliage in dense bunches. Zones 3–9.

# PICEA

*Spruce*

The 30 to 40 members of this genus of evergreen conifers originate in the cool-temperate regions of the northern hemisphere where there are deep pockets of moist, rich, acid, freely draining soil. Sometimes reaching an impressive 220 ft (66 m) in height, they develop a stiff, narrow, conical, sometimes columnar growth habit with short, horizontal to upward-pointing branches. The leaves are arranged spirally on short pegs and their color varies from bright green to glaucous blue. Able to withstand strong winds, they bear large cones which hang downward, distinguishing the genus from the superficially similar firs (*Abies*). The slow growth and contorted habit of some cultivars make them ideal bonsai specimens; others are prostrate and make excellent ground covers. This genus produces valuable timber, plus pitch and turpentine.

## Cultivation

Plant in full sun in deep, moist but well-drained neutral to acid soil. Propagate from seed or cuttings in autumn or by grafting. They will not survive transplantation when large, nor grow well in heavily polluted environments. They may be prone to attack from aphids, red spider mites and, in warm, humid climates, fungal infections.

### Picea omorika

**Serbian spruce**

From Serbia and Bosnia, this spruce reaches 100 ft (30 m) or more with pendulous branches forming a narrow, spire-like crown. The bright green flattened needles have a square tip and a grayish underside. The purplish cones mature to a deep brown. Happy in a range of soils from acid to limy and more tolerant of urban pollution than most species, it is one of the best *Picea* for large, temperate-climate gardens. *Picea omorika* × *breweriana* is a hybrid between the 2 popular, award-winning species. Zones 4–9.

### Picea pungens

**Colorado spruce**

This frost-hardy species from the west coast of the USA grows to 100 ft (30 m) or more in the wild, although less in gardens. It has a pyramid of bluish-green foliage composed of stiff and sharply pointed needles; the bark is gray. Prune regularly as fresh growth will not bud from dead wood. The many cultivars include '**Aurea**' with golden leaves; '**Caerulea**' with bluish-white leaves; '**Conica**', which

*Picea omorika*

*Pinus canariensis*

*Pinus densiflora*

grows into a cone-shaped cultivar; '**Glauca**', the commonly grown Colorado blue spruce with striking, steel-blue new foliage; '**Hoopsii**', prized for its even bluer foliage; '**Iseli Fastigiate**' with upward-pointing branches and very sharp needles; '**Koster**' with foliage maturing from silvery-deep blue to green, spiraled branches and tubular, scaled cones about 4 in (10 cm) long; '**Royal Blue**', another striking blue cultivar; '**Moerheimii**' with silvery-blue foliage longer than other forms; and '**Viridis**' with very dark green foliage. Zones 2–10.

# PINUS
Pine

Pines are arguably the most important genus of conifers. Consisting of around 120 species of needle-leafed evergreens, *Pinus* is represented in most parts of the northern hemisphere. The greatest concentration of species is in the Mexican highlands, southern USA and China—though the best-known species come from more northerly regions, for example, the Scots pine (*P. sylvestris*) of northern Eurasia. Most pines are medium to tall forest trees but a few are small and bushy. The characteristic feature of *Pinus* is the way the needles are grouped in bundles. The number per bundle, usually 2 to 7, is fairly constant for each species. Male (pollen) and female (seed) cones are borne on the same tree. Pines include many of the world's most important forest trees, providing lumber for many everyday purposes including house construction, and paper pulp. In the past their aromatic resins (pitch) and turpentines had many uses but these have largely been replaced by petroleum products. The seeds of several species (pine nuts) are important foods in some cultures. In recent times the bark of pines has become widely used in horticultural growing mediums and as a mulch.

## Cultivation

Most pines grow in a wide range of conditions, though their tolerance of both cold and warmth varies and each species has its optimum climate. They are mostly very wind resistant and will thrive on soils of moderate to low fertility, but may need a symbiotic soil fungus to assist nutrient uptake on poorer soils—these fungi are likely to be already present in the pines' native regions, but a handful of decaying needles from a pine forest can be added if planting pines where none has grown before. The majority of pines require well-drained soil, and resent soil disturbance. Propagation is from seed; cultivars may be grafted.

### *Pinus canariensis*

**Canary Islands pine**

This moderately fast-growing tree from the Canary Islands, though adaptable and tolerant of dry conditions, prefers an open, sunny spot where the soil is rich and moist yet well drained. It matures to a spreading tree, up to 80 ft (24 m) high. The upright trunk has reddish-brown, fissured bark. The densely packed, shiny, grass-green needles are 12 in (30 cm) long and are carried in groups of three. The oval, brown cones are 8 in (20 cm) long. Zones 8–11.

### *Pinus coulteri*

**Big-cone pine, Coulter pine**

This tough pine from California withstands heat, wind and dry conditions and tolerates most soils, including heavy clay. Its spiny brown cones grow to a massive 15 in (38 cm) and weigh 5 lb (2.3 kg). It grows fast to a bushy tree up to 90 ft (27 m) high with attractive, stiff, bluish-green needles up to 12 in (30 cm) long held in groups of three. Zones 8–10.

### *Pinus densiflora*

**Japanese red pine**

Used as a timber tree in its native Japan, where it can reach 100 ft (30 m), in cultivation this

Pinus patula

Pinus thunbergii

distinctive pine with red bark and a twisted shape is slow growing and often multi-trunked. It can be pruned and makes a popular bonsai specimen. Ovoid, yellow-purplish cones stand out boldly from the bright green, 4 in (10 cm) long foliage. There are many popular cultivars including '**Tanyosho Nana**'. The dwarf cultivar '**Umbraculifera**' has an umbrella-like canopy and orange-red, flaky bark on its multiple trunks; an extremely slow grower, it eventually reaches 15 ft (4.5 m). '**Pendula**' is a strong-growing, semi-prostrate cultivar best grown near ponds or on banks where its weeping form can be most appreciated. Zones 4–9.

### Pinus patula

**Mexican weeping pine, Spreading-leafed pine**

Long, slender, drooping needles and a spreading canopy make this a good shade tree. It is slow-growing to 50 ft (15 m) with a 15 ft (4.5 m) spread. The 8 in (20 cm) long needles are soft, pale green to grayish-green, and grouped in 3s; the oval cones are 4 in (10 cm) long. Zones 9–11.

### Pinus pinea

**Roman pine, Stone pine, Umbrella pine**

From southern Europe and Turkey, this species can reach 80 ft (24 m) in the wild and has a flattened crown atop a straight, though often leaning trunk with furrowed, reddish-gray bark. The rigid, paired needles, 4–8 in (10–20 cm) long, are bright green. The globe-shaped cones are shiny and brown; the edible seeds are known as pine nuts. Once established this pine copes with most conditions, including dryness and heat. Zones 8–10.

### Pinus sylvestris

**Scots pine**

This fast-growing species, found throughout northern Europe and western Asia (and the only pine indigenous to the UK), is the most commonly grown pine in Europe and is often used in forestry. It reaches 100 ft (30 m) with a rounded head of foliage and orange-red bark. Twisted, bluish-green needles grow in pairs and are 3 in (8 cm) long. This pine grows well in poor sandy soil but will not tolerate dry conditions. Dwarf cultivars make attractive tub specimens. '**Aurea**' has gold-tinted foliage, especially on new growth and in winter. '**Beuvronensis**' is a very densely foliaged dwarf cultivar with light blue-green needles that eventually reaches 6 ft (1.8 m) tall but is small for many years. '**Moseri**' is a small pyramidal cultivar with yellow foliage. '**Watereri**' only grows 2–3 in (5–8 cm) a year and can be thought of as a dwarf, blue-foliaged form of the Scots pine. It is ideal for rockeries or collections of dwarf conifers. Zones 4–9.

### Pinus thunbergii

syn. *Pinus thunbergiana*
**Japanese black pine**

This pine has a rugged trunk, purplish-black bark, pairs of thick needles, conspicuous white buds and an intricate framework of irregular, layered, horizontal branches. Widely grown in Japan as an ornamental, it has for centuries inspired artists and bonsai masters. It will stand any amount of pruning and trimming to shape; untrimmed it grows to 120 ft (36 m). It does very well in containers. '**Nishiki**' is a naturally dwarf, gnarled cultivar with corky bark very popular for bonsai. Zones 5–9.

## PITTOSPORUM

This genus consists of some 200 species of evergreen trees and shrubs from the tropical and subtropical regions of Australasia, Africa, Asia and the Pacific Islands. They make good specimen plants, screens and windbreaks or dense hedges in

*Pittosporum crassifolium*  *Pittosporum eugenioides*  *Pittosporum undulatum*

mild winter climates. The leaves are arranged alternately along the stems or in whorls. Several species have striking foliage prized by flower arrangers. The fragrant flowers are followed by fruits with a hard outer capsule enclosing round seeds with a sticky covering.

## Cultivation

Grow in fertile, well-drained soil and keep moist over summer to maintain the foliage at its best. They need full sun or part-shade, and a sheltered position in colder areas. Some species are frost tolerant and many are excellent for seaside gardens. Propagate from seed in autumn or spring, or from tip cuttings in summer.

### *Pittosporum crassifolium*

**Karo**

Native to New Zealand, this moderately frost hardy species grows to 25 ft (8 m) tall with a spread of 10 ft (3 m). The single trunk bears low-growing branches and a domed canopy. The oblong to oval leaves are dark green and leathery, 3 in (8 cm) long with grayish-white, felted undersides. Clusters of fragrant, star-shaped, reddish-purple flowers are borne in spring and are followed by fleshy, greenish-white, oval fruit up to 1 in (25 mm) long. Tolerant of dry conditions and suitable for seaside locations, it adapts to most soil types but needs an open, sunny aspect. '**Variegatum**' has gray to bright green leaves with an irregular cream edge. Zones 8–10.

### *Pittosporum eugenioides*

**Tarata, Lemonwood**

From New Zealand, this densely foliaged species is pyramidal when young and grows to 40 ft (12 m) tall with smooth, pale gray bark. The shiny, dark green, narrow, oval leaves have a wavy edge and a citrus-like aroma when crushed. The terminal clusters of small, star-shaped yellow flowers with a honey-like perfume appear in spring. Large clusters of green oval fruit follow, persisting through winter. Tolerant of both frost and dry conditions, it thrives in most soils if given an open, sunny spot. '**Variegatum**' has beautiful gray-green leaves blotched along the edge with white and grows 8–15 ft (2.4–4.5 m) tall. The species and its cultivars are suitable for clipped hedges. Zones 9–11.

### *Pittosporum undulatum*

**Sweet pittosporum, Australian daphne**

This popular Australian species reaches 20–40 ft (6–12 m) tall with a wide dome. The dense green leaves are lance-shaped with scalloped edges. Profuse clusters of creamy white, bell-shaped flowers in spring are followed by yellow-brown fruit. Marginally frost hardy, it prefers moderate to warm climates. Watch for white scale and sooty mold. '**Sunburst**' is a popular cultivar. Zones 9–11.

## PLATANUS

Plane, Sycamore

This genus consists of 6 species of large, vigorous, wide-crowned, deciduous trees from Eurasia, North America and Mexico. It contains some of the world's largest shade trees for dry-summer climates, many of which are widely used as street trees. They are called planes or plane trees in some countries, sycamores in others. The most conspicuous feature is the flaking, mottled bark, which is shed in winter. The 5-lobed leaves are large and maple-like, and the brown seed balls hang in clusters on the trees in winter. The flowers are insignificant.

## Cultivation

They thrive in deep, rich, well-drained soil in a sunny site and can be transplanted. Propagate from seed or cuttings or by layering. Most tolerate

*Platanus × acerifolia* — *Platanus orientalis* (leaf) — *Platanus orientalis*

severe pruning, air pollution and hard construction (such as paving) covering the roots.

### *Platanus × acerifolia*

**syns** *Platanus × hispanica, P. × hybrida*
**London plane**

A good street tree, this fast-growing hybrid grows to 120 ft (36 m). It withstands poor conditions and is resistant to leaf blight; however, the roots can lift paving and the large leaves can block small drains. Its straight, erect trunk is attractively blotched in gray, brown and white. Zones 3–10.

### *Platanus orientalis*

**Chinar, chennar, Oriental plane**

Ranging from Turkey to the western Himalayas, this large tree grows about 100 ft (30 m) tall with spreading branches. Fully frost hardy, it has a relatively short, stout trunk and flaking gray to greenish-white bark. Its deeply incised leaves form 5 to 7 narrow, pointed lobes, and 3 to 5 round, brown seed heads hang like beads on a thread. It is used as a street tree in Australia, southern Africa and southern Europe. The leaves of '**Digitata**' have elongated, narrow lobes that are more deeply cut. Zones 3–10.

## PLUMERIA

*Frangipani, Temple tree*

*Plumeria* commemorates Charles Plumier, a seventeenth-century French botanist who described several tropical species. The genus contains 8 species of mainly deciduous shrubs and trees, originally from Central America, known for their strongly fragrant flowers. The trees can reach 30 ft (9 m), though they are generally much smaller. Their fleshy branches contain a poisonous, milky sap. In the tropics, the terminally held flowers (generally white) appear before the leaves and continue to flower for most of the year. In subtropical climates the flowers appear in spring, after the leaves, and continue growing until the next winter. The fruits consist of 2 leathery follicles, although the trees rarely fruit in cultivation. Most plumerias in gardens are hybrids.

### Cultivation

In colder climates, these trees and shrubs can be grown in a greenhouse. Outdoors, they prefer full sun and moderately fertile, well-drained soil. Propagate in early spring from cuttings that have been allowed to dry out for a couple of weeks.

### *Plumeria rubra*

This popular, deciduous small tree, with its broadly rounded canopy, grows to 25 ft (8 m) tall. Distinguished by its pale pink to crimson flowers, it is used extensively for decoration. **Plumeria rubra var. *acutifolia*** features creamy white flowers, sometimes flushed pink, with a deep yellow center. '**Golden Kiss**' has large heads of golden-yellow flowers with a soft flush of apricot-pink edging each petal. Zones 10–12.

## PODOCARPUS

*Plum pine*

From the wet tropics and southern hemisphere continents extending also to Japan and Mexico, the 100 or so species are all moderately fast-growing evergreens, ranging from 3 ft (1 m) ground covers to 150 ft (45 m) trees. They are grown for their dense foliage and attractive habit. The flat, generally narrow leaves are spirally arranged. Male and female plants are separate: males having catkin-like yellow pollen cones; females having naked seeds held on short stalks that develop into the fleshy blue-black to red berry-like 'fruits' that give them their common name. Some species are harvested for softwood.

*Opposite: Platanus × acerifolia*

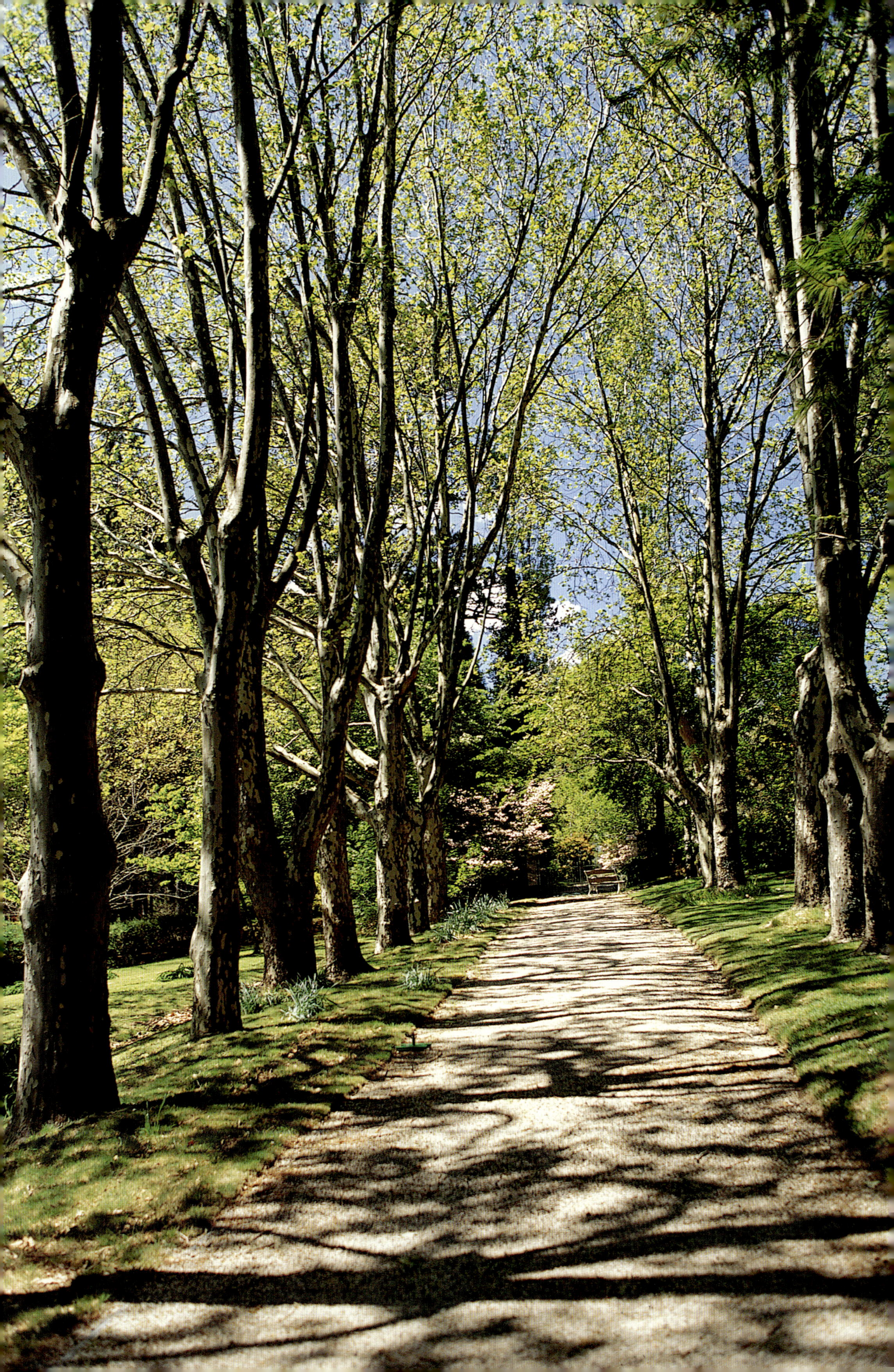

*Podocarpus macrophyllus*

*Populus deltoides*

## Cultivation

Although warm-temperate climates, free from heavy frost, suit them best, they grow in a range of soils and in full sun or part-shade, depending on the species. In cooler areas, they grow indoors. Leave unpruned unless a hedge is desired. Propagate from seed or cuttings.

### Podocarpus macrophyllus

**Kusamaki, Buddhist pine, Yew pine**

From mountainous Japan and China, where it grows to 70 ft (21 m) tall with a spread of 12 ft (3.5 m), this cold-tolerant species prefers moist, rich soil. It has long, thick, dark green leaves up to 6 in (15 cm) long and responds well to pruning, making a good thick hedge. Often grown in Japanese temple gardens, it is suitable for containers. Berries are small and black. '**Maki**', rarely bigger than a shrub, has an erect habit with almost vertical branches. Zones 7–11.

### Podocarpus totara

**Totara, Mahogany pine**

Slow-growing to a height of 100 ft (30 m), this New Zealand tree is one of the tallest of the genus and can live for much more than 200 years. Its trunk grows to a diameter of 10 ft (3 m) and yields a valuable timber. Its dense, sharp-pointed leaves are stiff and bronze-green; fresh reddish-brown bark matures to grayish-brown before peeling off in strips. Round crimson fruit, about ½ in (12 mm) in diameter, are carried on red stalks. Zones 9–11.

## POPULUS

*Poplar, Aspen, Cottonwood*

This genus of some 35 species of fast-growing, deciduous trees is from temperate regions of the northern hemisphere. In autumn many blaze with yellow or gold. Cultivated in parks, large gardens and as avenue trees, windbreaks and screens, their soft white timber is used for making matches and packing cases. Male and female flowers, borne on separate trees, are hanging catkins and appear in late winter and early spring before the leaves, which are set on long, flexible stalks. The fruits are capsules containing seeds covered with cotton-like hairs. Most species live only 60 years or so.

## Cultivation

Plant in deep, moist, well-drained, fertile soil in full sun; they dislike arid conditions. Many species have vigorous root systems that block drains and lift paving, and so are not suitable for small gardens; some species sucker freely from the roots. Propagate from cuttings in winter.

### Populus deltoides

**Eastern cottonwood, Eastern poplar**

An upright, broad-headed tree from eastern North America growing to 100 ft (30 m), this species is less likely to sucker than other poplars. It is short-lived and brittle in high winds. The triangular, glossy green leaves are up to 8 in (20 cm) long and are coarsely toothed; the bark is gray and deeply corrugated. The long catkins are yellow and red. The name cottonwood refers to the fluff that surrounds the seeds. This is a tough tree for extreme inland conditions. ***Populus deltoides* var. *monilifera***, the northern cottonwood, bears slightly smaller leaves with the toothed margins more sharply delineated. Zones 3–11.

### Populus nigra

**Black poplar**

At 100 ft (30 m), with a suckering habit, this tree is not for small gardens. It has dark, deeply

*Podocarpus totara*

*Sweet cherry bears profuse white flowers in late spring, followed by black-red fruit.*

Populus tremula

Prunus avium 'Plena'

furrowed bark. Its large, diamond-shaped leaves, bronze when young, become bright green, then yellow in autumn; held on thin stalks, they seem to 'dance' perpetually. Male trees produce black catkins in mid-winter. Best known of the many cultivars is '**Italica**' (syn. *Populus pyramidalis*), the Lombardy poplar, a male cultivar popular for its narrow, columnar shape and fast growth. Zones 6–10.

### Populus tremula

**Common aspen, European aspen**

A vigorous, spreading tree from Europe suitable for cool climates, this species grows to about 50 ft (15 m). The rounded, toothed leaves are bronze-red when young, gray-green in maturity and turn a clear yellow in autumn. They are held on slim, flat stems and quiver and rustle in the slightest breeze. Long gray catkins are carried in late winter. In large gardens and parks constant mowing will control its suckering habit Zones 1–9.

## PRUNUS

This large genus of some 430 species, mostly from the northern hemisphere, includes the edible stone fruits—cherries, plums, apricots, peaches, nectarines and almonds—but there are also ornamental species and cultivars with beautiful flowers. The genus includes several shrubby species, but most are trees growing on average to 15 ft (4.5 m), although some can reach 100 ft (30 m). Most of the familiar species are deciduous and bloom in spring (or late winter in mild climates) with scented, 5-petalled, pink or white flowers. The leaves are simple and often serrated, and all produce a fleshy fruit containing a single hard stone. Many have attractive autumn foliage, and others have interesting bark. Cherry and plum timber is sometimes used commercially.

### Cultivation

Plant in moist, well-drained soil in full sun but with protection from strong wind for the spring blossom. Keep the base of trees free of weeds and long grass. Feed young trees with a high-nitrogen fertilizer. Many fruiting varieties respond well to espaliering. Propagate by grafting or from seed—named cultivars must be grafted or budded onto seedling stocks. Pests and diseases vary with locality.

### Prunus avium

**Sweet cherry, Gean, Mazzard, Wild cherry**

Native to Europe and western Asia, this species is the major parent of the cultivated sweet cherries. It can reach 60 ft (18 m) tall, with a rounded crown and a stout, straight trunk with banded reddish-brown bark. The pointed, dark green leaves are up to 6 in (15 cm) long and turn red, crimson and yellow before they drop. Profuse white flowers appear in late spring before the leaves and are followed by black-red fruit. The cultivated cherries are rarely self-fertile, so trees of 2 or more different clones are often necessary for fruit production. Cherry wood is prone to fungus, so avoid pruning in winter or in wet weather. The ornamental cultivar '**Plena**' carries a mass of drooping, double white flowers. Zones 3–9.

### Prunus campanulata

**Taiwan cherry, Carmine cherry**

This species from Taiwan, south China and the Ryukyu Islands is less frost tolerant than most deciduous *Prunus* species and likes warm-temperate climates. It can grow to 30 ft (9 m) but is mostly smaller in cultivation. Cherries bloom in mid- to late winter in a warm climate, or early spring in cooler climates. The bare branches are festooned with clusters of bell-shaped flowers, bright carmine red in the commonly grown form. The foliage turns bronze-red in autumn. Like most cherries, it responds poorly to pruning. Zones 7–11.

Prunus cerasifera

Prunus sargentii

## Prunus cerasifera

**Cherry plum, Myrobalan, Purple-leafed plum**

Native to Turkey and the Caucasus region, this small-fruited, thornless plum has long been cultivated in Europe. It grows to about 30 ft (9 m) and is tolerant of dry conditions, with an erect, bushy habit and smallish leaves that are slightly bronze-tinted. Profuse, small white flowers appear before the leaves, in spring in cool climates and in late winter in milder ones, followed by edible red plums up to $1\frac{1}{4}$ in (30 mm) in diameter in summer. This species has many ornamental cultivars, the most widely grown being those with deep purple foliage. '**Nigra**' has vibrant, deep-purple leaves turning more blackish-purple in late summer; in spring it bears single, pale pink blossoms with a red calyx and stamens. The cherry-sized red fruit are edible but sour. '**Elvins**' is an Australian-raised cultivar grown for its white blossom, prettily flushed with flesh pink, which is densely massed on arching branches in mid-spring; it grows only to about 12 ft (3.5 m). Zones 3–10.

## Prunus mume

**Japanese apricot**

Closely related to the common apricot, this very early flowering species is a native of China but has been cultivated for many centuries in both China and Japan, where it has given rise to hundreds of named cultivars selected for both fruit and flower. It makes a round-headed tree of 15–30 ft (4.5–9 m) high with sharply pointed leaves up to 4 in (10 cm) long. The lightly scented, white to deep pink flowers, 1 in (25 mm) or more across, are carried in small clusters along the branches in late spring; yellowish, apricot-like fruit follow. Its blossoms feature in classical Chinese and Japanese paintings and it is also popular for bonsai work. Cultivars include '**Albo-plena**' with white double flowers; '**Beni-chidori**', a later flowerer with fragrant pink double flowers; '**Pendula**' with a weeping habit; and '**Geisha**' with semi-double deep rose flowers. Zones 6–9.

## Prunus sargentii

**Sargent cherry**

This flowering cherry species, native to Japan, Korea and eastern Siberia, is one of the tallest of the Japanese flowering cherry group, growing to as much as 80 ft (24 m), with dark chestnut-colored bark. In mid-spring the branches are covered with pink flowers with deeper pink stamens, accompanied by the unfolding leaves, which are long-pointed and up to 5 in (12 cm) in length; in autumn they make a brilliant display of reddish-bronze, turning orange and red. This species performs best away from polluted environments. Zones 4–9.

## Prunus, Sato-zakura Group

This is the main group of Japanese flowering cherries, believed to be derived mainly from the species *Prunus serrulata* (under which name they are commonly found), but with probable hybrid influence of several closely related species. Mostly small to medium-sized trees, they can be recognized by their large leaves with fine, even teeth ending in bristle-like points, and their loose umbels of flowers that are mostly over $1\frac{1}{2}$ in (35 mm) in diameter; the bases of the umbels carry conspicuous toothed bracts, like miniature leaves. They are among the most widely planted trees for spring blossom in cool climates but require good rainfall and a mild summer for the best display of blossom. The numerous cultivars are mostly of Japanese origin and there has been much confusion as to their names. Height and growth form vary with cultivar, as do the color, shape and size of the flowers and the color of the new leaves, which unfold with or just after the opening flowers. '**Amanogawa**' has a narrow habit, growing to 30 ft

*Prunus × subhirtella*

*Prunus*, Sato-zakura Group 'Sekiyama'

(9 m) high, and carries fragrant, semi-double white to shell-pink flowers. '**Sekiyama**' (syn. 'Kanzan'), a vigorous grower to 10 ft (3 m), bears double purple-pink flowers in mid-spring. '**Cheal's Weeping**' (syn. 'Kiku-shidare') flowers early, carrying double deep pink flowers on weeping branches. '**Shirotae**' (syn. 'Mount Fuji'), growing to 20 ft (6 m), has slightly drooping, spreading branches; green, lacy-edged leaves appear in early spring and turn orange-red in autumn; in mid-spring it carries a wealth of fragrant, single or semi-double white blossoms. '**Okumiyako**' (syn. 'Shimidsu sakura'), growing to 15 ft (4.5 m), has wide, spreading branches; pink-tinted buds appear in late spring and open to fringed, large, double white flowers, and the leaves turn orange and red in autumn. '**Pink Perfection**' is a strong-growing cultivar with clusters of large deep pink, double flowers that open from red buds. '**Shirofugen**', strong-growing to 20 ft (6 m), blooms late, and the purplish-pink buds intermingle attractively with the young, copper leaves; clusters of double flowers open white and turn purplish-pink. '**Shogetsu**' makes a 15 ft (4.5 m), spreading tree with arching branches and large clusters of semi-double to fully double, white-centered, pale pink flowers; it blooms late. '**Taihaku**', known as the great white cherry, is a vigorous, spreading tree to 20 ft (6 m) or more; in mid-spring it bears large, pure-white flowers and bronze-red young leaves that mature to dark green. '**Takasago**', the Naden cherry, with scented pink flowers, is thought by some to be a hybrid with *P. × yedoensis*. '**Ukon**', an upright tree to 30 ft (9 m), bears large pink-tinged, greenish-cream flowers in mid-spring. Zones 5–9.

## Prunus serrula

### Tibetan cherry

Native to western China, this deciduous, neatly round-headed tree growing to 50 ft (15 m) is prized in gardens for its gleaming, mahogany red bark. Clusters of small white flowers appear in spring at the same time as the new leaves, which mature to dark green and turn yellow in autumn; the tiny round fruit are red to black. This species requires a cool climate. Zones 5–9.

## Prunus × subhirtella

### Higan cherry, Rosebud cherry

This graceful cherry from Japan is now believed to be of hybrid origin. It grows to 30 ft (9 m) and produces a profusion of pale pink flowers in early spring. The leaves are dark green and pointed, and fade to shades of yellow before dropping. It thrives in cool climates but can be rather short-lived. '**Autumnalis**', growing to 15 ft (4.5 m), bears pink-budded white flowers intermittently from late autumn through winter and into early spring; '**Autumnalis Rosea**' is similar but has pale pink flowers. '**Pendula**' has slender, vertically pendulous branches like a weeping willow and is usually grafted onto a standard; it bears a profusion of small pale pink, 5-petalled flowers from late winter into spring, followed by little spherical brown-red fruit. The spring-blooming '**Pendula Rubra**' bears rich pink flowers. '**Accolade**' makes a spreading tree to about 25 ft (8 m) with quite large pale pink semi-double flowers opening from deep pink buds in early spring. '**Hally Jolivette**' is a large shrub, growing to 8–15 ft (2.4–4.5 m) in height and spread with many reddish, upright stems covered for 2 to 3 weeks in spring with double white flowers opening from pink buds. Zones 5–9.

## Prunus × yedoensis

### Tokyo cherry, Yoshino cherry

This is another Japanese cherry that is now regarded as a hybrid, the parents probably *Prunus speciosa* and *P. × subhirtella*. It is a small tree, growing quite rapidly to 30 ft (9 m) high and wide. Massed fragrant white or pale pink flowers usually open before the new foliage develops; the deep green

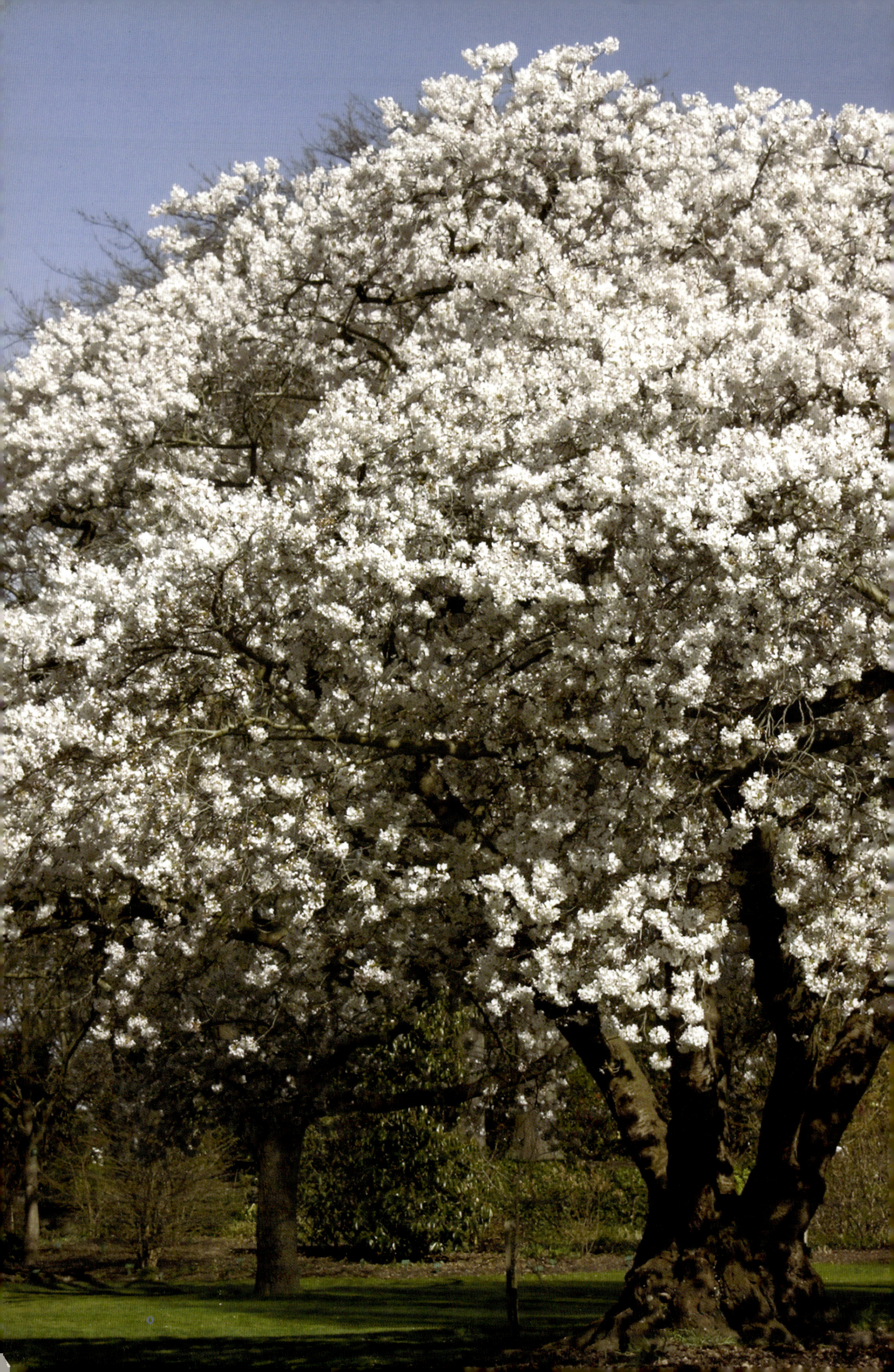

*Pseudopanax crassifolius* — *Pseudopanax laetus*

4 in (10 cm) long leaves color well in autumn. It makes a beautiful lawn specimen or avenue tree and is the main flowering cherry planted in Washington DC. '**Ivensii**' has an arching and weeping growth habit. '**Akebono**' has pure pink flowers. '**Shidare Yoshino**' has a weeping habit and masses of pure white flowers. Zones 5–9.

# Pseudopanax

syns *Neopanax, Nothopanax*

Members of this small genus of evergreen trees and shrubs are grown for their interesting fruits and foliage. Most of the 12 to 20 species are endemic to New Zealand with one each in Tasmania, New Caledonia and Chile. The leaves are simple when young, becoming compound as they mature. The 5-petalled, greenish summer flowers are inconspicuous. They are followed by clusters of berries. These plants make good tub specimens and attractive house plants.

## Cultivation
Suited to warm-climate gardens, they need well-drained soil enriched with humus either in sun or part-shade. Propagate from seed or cuttings taken in summer.

### Pseudopanax crassifolius

**Horoeka, Lancewood**

This small tree from New Zealand changes dramatically with age. Young plants have a single stem up to 8 ft (2.4 m) tall. The stiff, sword-like, narrow leaves, up to 3 ft (1 m) long, are dark shiny green above, purplish beneath, with sharply serrated edges and a reddish midrib. Older plants are branched, 30 ft (9 m) or so tall with a rounded canopy 10 ft (3 m) wide. The leaves then become compound, with leathery leaflets 12 in (30 cm) long and edges more deeply toothed. Small, black, ornamental fruit are produced by female plants. Zones 9–11.

### Pseudopanax laetus

Ultimately up to 20 ft (6 m) tall, this species is widely grown as a tub plant when young. It has luxuriant hand-shaped leaves with 5 to 7 leaflets, each of which is up to 10 in (25 cm) long. New leaf buds are enclosed in a jelly and open from purplish young stems. The large heads of tiny green flowers are followed by small purple-red seed capsules. This is a great plant for adding a tropical touch to a temperate garden. Zones 9–10.

# Pseudotsuga

Among the largest of all conifers, the 6 to 8 *Pseudotsuga* species are seldom seen at their maximum height outside their native North America, China, Taiwan, Japan and Mexico. They can reach 300 ft (90 m) with a cylindrical trunk supporting an attractive, broad pyramidal shape. The leaves are soft, green, flattened and tapered, with two bands of white on their undersides. The brown cones, 2 in (5 cm) long with pointed bracts, hang downward; they take a year to mature.

## Cultivation
These very frost-hardy trees prefer cold climates, cool, deep soil and sunny, open spaces. Propagate from seed or by grafting.

### Pseudotsuga menziesii

syns *Pseudotsuga douglasii, P. taxifolia*
**Douglas fir, Oregon pine**

This fast-growing conifer can reach 300 ft (90 m). Very long-lived, some specimens have reached the age of 400 years. Its timber has long been valued in North America. Its sturdy trunk is covered with dark, reddish-brown, thick, corky bark. The branch

Opposite: *Prunus × yedoensis* 'Shidare Yoshino'

*Pseudotsuga menziesii*          *Pterocarya carpinifolia*          *Pterostyrax hispida*

tips curve upward and have dense, soft, fragrant, bluish-green, needle-like foliage. At each branch tip wine-red buds form in winter, opening as apple-green rosettes of new growth in spring. Pendulous cones appear after the plant is 20 years old. Zones 4–9.

## PTEROCARYA

*Wing nut*

Ranging from the Caucasus to China, this genus consists of about 10 species of deciduous trees that are grown for their handsome leaves and pendent flowers. Reaching a height of 100 ft (30 m) or more, they have spreading crowns with abundant, pinnate, bright green leaves, each leaflet 4 in (10 cm) or more long. Members can be readily identified by the spring flowers, which appear as yellowish-green catkins and grow to 18 in (45 cm) long. Winged nutlets, forming chains up to 18 in (45 cm) long, hang from the branches in ribbons and are an eye-catching feature.

### Cultivation

These very frost-hardy trees prefer full sun and fertile, deep, moist but well-drained soil. Propagate from cuttings in summer or from suckers or seed in autumn.

### Pterocarya carpinifolia

The name of this species means 'with leaves like *Carpinus*' (the hornbeam genus). This presumably refers to the conspicuous, regular veining of the leaflets—though the hornbeams, of course, differ in having simple, not compound leaves. In other respects *Pterocarya carpinifolia* resembles *P. fraxinifolia*. Zones 5–9.

### Pterocarya fraxinifolia

**Caucasian wing nut**

This large tree quickly reaches 100 ft (30 m) and has a wide crown adorned with numerous leaflets. Its flowers form long, pendulous, greenish-golden catkins; these are followed by ribbons of winged fruit. This species needs a sheltered position and is an excellent shade tree for a large garden or park, especially near water. Zones 5–9.

## PTEROSTYRAX

This genus from Asia consists of 4 species of deciduous shrubs and trees that reach up to 50 ft (15 m) with a spread of 40 ft (12 m). The slender branches carry serrated leaves, which are 6 in (15 cm) or more long, bright green and oval. Creamy white, fluffy flowers are produced in pendulous sprays up to 10 in (25 cm) long. The fruit is in the form of bristly seed capsules.

### Cultivation

Plant in deep, moist, well-drained soil in sun or part-shade. Propagate from seed in the cooler months, from cuttings in summer or by layering. These useful shade trees should be pruned only to control shape and size.

### Pterostyrax hispida

**Epaulette tree, Fragrant epaulette tree**

This species from China and Japan grows to 50 ft (15 m). Rich green, oval leaves with wedge-shaped bases and downy undersides form a dense crown. In summer it displays fragrant white flowers in drooping sprays. Gray, furry, 10-ribbed fruit appears in early autumn and stays on the bare branches during winter. Zones 4–9.

## PYRUS

*Pear*

These 30 or so species from temperate Eurasia and North Africa are related to the apple (*Malus*). Slow-growing, deciduous and semi-evergreen trees, they

*Pyrus salicifolia* 'Pendula'

*Quercus coccinea*

can reach 80 ft (24 m) but are often smaller. Cultivated since antiquity for their grainy textured, sweet, juicy, yellowish-green fruits, not all of which are pear-shaped, they are also valued for their attractive autumn foliage, which needs plenty of sun, and their clusters of fragrant, 5-petalled, white flowers, sometimes tinged pink, which appear with the leaves, or just before them, in spring. The glossy leaves vary from almost round to quite narrow.

## Cultivation

Having modest moisture needs, they suit coastal areas with heavy, sandy loams and good drainage in a sunny position. They are ideal for cool-temperate climates. Cross-pollinate for fruit. Prune to remove damaged branches and for shape in late winter or early spring. Propagate from seed or by grafting.

### *Pyrus salicifolia*

**Willow-leafed pear, Silver pear, Weeping silver pear**

This popular ornamental pear, to about 25 ft (8 m), comes from the Caucasus and Iran. Graceful, arching branches have long, silver-gray willow-like foliage covered with silky down when young. Small, creamy-white flowers are often hidden by the foliage. The small, brown, pear-shaped fruit ripen in autumn. '**Pendula**' has a willowy habit and is more popular than the species itself; its foliage is smaller than that of its parent. Both are very frost hardy. Zones 4–9.

## QUERCUS
*Oak*

Most oaks are from temperate regions but some of the 600 or so evergreen, semi-evergreen and deciduous species are from tropical and subtropical regions of Mexico, Southeast Asia and New Guinea. Oaks range from shrubs 3 ft (1 m) high to trees of 120 ft (36 m), and are long-lived; some species have been used for centuries for hardwood timber. Their leaves, mostly lobed and leathery, but in some species thin and lustrous, make good compost for acid-loving plants. The leaves of some deciduous oaks develop magnificent hues during the cooler months before they drop. Oaks divide into 'white oaks', with rounded leaf lobes and edible acorns that mature in one year, and 'red oaks', with pointed leaf lobes and acorns that mature in 2 years and are too bitter to eat. Female flowers are insignificant and greenish, but male flowers appear as yellow catkins in spring.

## Cultivation

They thrive in deep, damp, well-drained soil. Some species like full sun; others prefer part-shade when young. They have extensive root systems and do not like to be transplanted. Prune only to remove damaged limbs. Oaks are susceptible to oak-leaf miner in humid climates, as well as oak root fungus and aphids. Propagate from fresh seed or by grafting in late winter just before new buds appear.

### *Quercus coccinea*

**Scarlet oak**

This deciduous eastern North American oak has deeply lobed, glossy bright green leaves with bristly tips. The 6 in (15 cm) long leaves turn brilliant scarlet in a cool, dry autumn and stay on the tree for a long time. It reaches 80 ft (24 m) on a strong central trunk and is distinguished by its drooping branches. The bark is gray and darkens as it matures. *Quercus coccinea* can tolerate pollution and makes a good specimen for urban environments. '**Splendens**' has very deep red autumn foliage color. Zones 2–9.

### *Quercus ilex*

**Holm oak, Holly oak**

Native to southern Europe and North Africa, near the Mediterranean coast, this round-headed,

*Quercus robur* 'Fastigiata'

*Quercus rubra*

## TREES

dense evergreen grows to 90 ft (27 m). Its leaves may be toothed (similar to holly) or entire, and are silver-gray at first, becoming a lustrous dark green above, white and downy underneath with age. It grows well in an exposed position, particularly on the coast, and makes a good windbreak. Zones 7–10.

### Quercus palustris

**Pin oak**

From the eastern and central USA, this species tolerates dry, sandy soil though it is at its best in deep alluvial soils with plenty of water in summer. Moderately fast-growing, it matures to 80 ft (24 m) high. Its lustrous green leaves are 4 in (10 cm) long with deep, pointed lobes that turn crimson in autumn and persist on the tree well into winter. It has a shallow root system. Zones 3–10.

### Quercus robur

**Common oak, English oak, Pedunculate oak**

Arguably the most famous of all the oaks and with a life span of 600 to 700 years, this species has spreading, densely leafed branches that provide good shade. Its 4 in (10 cm) long leaves are deciduous and remain dark green through autumn. It reaches a height of 120 ft (36 m) and trunks with a circumference of more than 70 ft (21 m) have been recorded. It is one of Europe's most valuable timber trees. '**Fastigiata**' is grown for its narrow, upright habit. Zones 3–10.

### Quercus rubra

**syn. *Quercus borealis***
**Red oak, Northern red oak**

Originating in eastern USA and eastern Canada, this robust deciduous tree reaches up to 90 ft (27 m) with a broad canopy formed by strong, straight branches. The matt green leaves with pointed lobes are up to 8 in (20 cm) in length and display rich scarlet and red-brown autumn hues. The large acorn is held in a shallow cup. The red oak grows relatively quickly and does well in sun or part-shade. The young leaves of '**Aurea**' are bright yellow. Zones 3–9.

### Quercus suber

**Cork oak**

The thick, furrowed, gray bark of *Quercus suber*, principally from Spain and Portugal and growing elsewhere around the Mediterranean, is the source of commercial cork. It reaches 60 ft (18 m) high with a broad, spreading canopy of 50 ft (15 m). The oval, evergreen leaves with a slightly toothed edge are up to 3 in (8 cm) long; they are a dark, shiny green on top and silvery beneath. Single or paired acorns mature to chocolate brown and are held loosely in a cup covering just over a third of the acorn. Zones 8–10.

## RHODODENDRON

**syn. *Azalea***

The rhododendrons are a spectacular genus of around 800 evergreen, semi-deciduous and deciduous species largely confined to the northern hemisphere with the majority of species native to southern China and the Himalayan region and many in North America, Japan and Southeast Asia. Although better known as shrubs, many of the species and some of the gardens hybrids and cultivars will become tree-like with age. Rhododendrons are grown mainly for their massed display of flowers, which appear mainly in spring and which vary greatly in size from tiny thimbles to 8 in (20 cm) trumpets. They are usually clustered in inflorescences (trusses) at the branch tips and occur in every color except a true bright blue. The flowers may be self- or multi-colored, often with a

*The rhododendrons are a spectacular genus of around 800 evergreen, semi-deciduous and deciduous species grown mainly for their mass display of flowers, which appear mainly in spring*

*Rhododendron arboreum*

*Rhododendron sinogrande*

contrasting throat blotch (flare) or spotting. Some species have scented flowers. Rhododendrons also have beautiful foliage. The leaves are usually thick and leathery, often deep green and lustrous. Leaf size varies enormously and the foliage of species from mild, high rainfall areas can exceed 24 in (60 cm) long. Some rhododendrons have felting (indumentum) on the foliage, usually confined to the leaf undersides.

## Cultivation

As would be expected of such a large group, rhododendrons vary considerably in their climatic preferences. However, they all share the same general cultivation needs. This is because their roots lack the fine feeding hairs at the root tips that are found on most other plants; instead, the entire root ball is a mass of fine roots that serves the same function as root hairs. Fine roots dry out quickly in dry conditions, soon rot if kept waterlogged, suffer in compacted soils and cannot penetrate hard or rocky ground. Rhododendrons need loose, open, well-aerated, acid soil with plenty of humus to retain moisture. Most rhododendrons are woodland plants that prefer dappled shade or at least protection from the hottest afternoon sun and strong winds. They are not greatly troubled by pests and diseases but are prone to infestation by thrips, two-spotted mites and spider mites and powdery mildew or rust in humid areas. Rhododendrons are propagated from seed or cuttings or by layering, the method and timing varying with the type of plant.

### Rhododendron arboreum

From northern India to southern China and over 100 ft (30 m) tall in the wild, this species reaches 40 ft (12 m) in cultivation with a narrow, cylindrical crown. Its leathery, bronze-green, 8 in (20 cm) long leaves have whitish or rust-colored undersides. Red, white or deep pink bell-shaped flowers in globular heads of 15 to 20 blooms open in very early spring. This species was an early introduction and is a parent of many cultivars. Zones 7–11.

### Rhododendron elliottii

Native to moderate altitudes in northern India, this species grows to 6–25 ft (1.8–8 m) tall and has deep red flowers with very dark spotting and white-tipped anthers. The flowers open from mid-spring, are funnel- to bell-shaped, around 2 in (5 cm) long and in trusses of around 10 blooms. The leaves are glossy deep green and up to 4 in (10 cm) long. Zones 9–10.

### Rhododendron macabeanum

This species from northern India is a tree up to 50 ft (15 m) tall. It has very dark green, heavily veined, leathery leaves up to 18 in (45 cm) long with white indumentum on the undersides. Pale yellow, bell-shaped, 2–3 in (5–8 cm) long flowers with a basal purple blotch are carried in rounded trusses of up to 20 blooms and open from early spring. Zones 8–9.

### Rhododendron sinogrande

This evergreen rhododendron is distinctive for its huge, glossy green leaves that reach 32 in (80 cm) in length and 12 in (30 cm) in width, and are silvery underneath. These are matched in spring by enormous trusses of bell-shaped, creamy white to yellow flowers with crimson blotches. Growing to a height of 40 ft (13 m), it needs a sheltered spot and a cool but mild climate. Zones 8–10.

## ROBINIA
*Black locust*

These 20 species of leguminous deciduous shrubs and trees from the USA are fast-growing and

*Robinia pseudoacacia* — *Robinia pseudoacacia* 'Frisia' — *Salix alba* 'Britzensis'

tolerate pollution. Some grow 80 ft (24 m) tall but many are shrub-like, reaching only 6 ft (1.8 m). Most spread by suckers and self-seed. The pinnate leaves, usually with a pair of spines at each base, have small oval leaflets, sometimes turning buttery yellow in autumn. They bear pendulous sprays of pink, purple or white, fragrant pea-blossoms in spring. Fruits are flat pods less than 4 in (10 cm). Cultivars have been grafted to produce a mop-like head of foliage.

## Cultivation

Robinias prefer poor but moist soil in a sunny position sheltered from strong winds. Propagate from scarified seed, cuttings or suckers or by division. Cultivars must be grafted.

### Robinia hispida

**Rose acacia**

*Robinia hispida* is a deciduous shrub from the dry woods and scrub of southeastern USA. It has pinnate leaves that are fresh green, long and fern-like; the erect stems and branches are clothed in brown bristles. In summer, rose-pink pea-flowers are followed by bristly seed pods up to 3 in (8 cm) long. In favorable conditions the plant quickly reaches 6 ft (1.8 m). This species is sometimes grafted on to stems of *R. pseudoacacia* to produce a small, mop-headed tree. On **Robinia hispida var. kelseyi** (syn. *R. kelseyi*) only the flower stalks and raceme axes have bristles; it bears glossy rose-pink flowers. Zones 5–10.

### Robinia pseudoacacia

**False acacia, Black locust**

This fast-growing 80 ft (24 m) tree has dark, deeply grooved bark and prickly branches. The pinnate, fern-like leaves, with about 23 leaflets, turn yellow in autumn. Scented white pea-flowers appear in late spring or summer, followed by reddish-brown pods with black, kidney-shaped seeds. The cultivar '**Frisia**' carries golden foliage deepening in autumn. '**Rozynskiana**' is a small tree with drooping branches and leaves. '**Tortuosa**' has short, twisted branches. '**Umbraculifera**', the mop-head acacia, is also thornless and rarely flowers. These cultivars rarely exceed 30 ft (9 m). Zones 3–10.

## SALIX

Willow, Osier, sallow

This genus includes about 300 species of deciduous trees, shrubs and subshrubs mainly from cold and temperate regions in the northern hemisphere. The fast-growing but relatively short-lived trees are the most widely grown, mainly for their timber, their twigs which are used in basket-making and their strong suckering habit, which aids soil retention. Willow bark was the original source of aspirin. The leaves are usually bright green, lance-shaped and narrow. The flowers, which are borne in fluffy catkins, are conspicuous in some species, appearing before or with the new leaves; male and female catkins are usually borne on separate trees.

## Cultivation

These frost-hardy plants do best in areas with clearly defined seasons and prefer cool, moist soil with sun or part-shade. Propagation is from seed or cuttings in either winter or summer, or by layering. They are vulnerable to attack by caterpillars, aphids and gall mites as well as canker-causing fungal diseases.

### Salix alba

**White willow**

A very adaptable tree from Europe, northern Africa and central Asia, this species grows to about 80 ft (24 m) high. Its erect branches weep somewhat at the tips and are clothed with 3 in (8 cm) long, narrow leaves that are bright green above with

**Opposite:** *Salix babylonica*

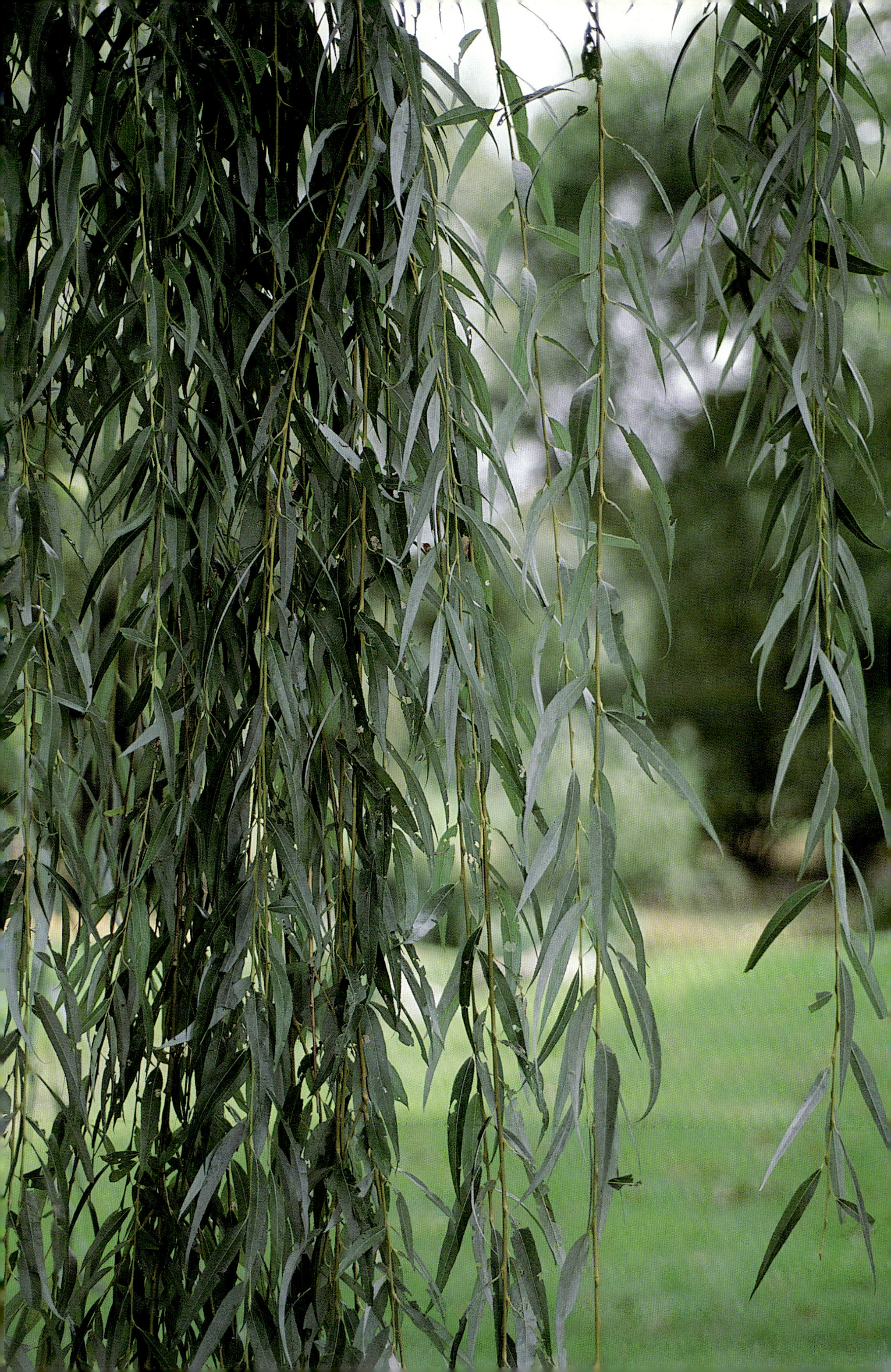

*Schefflera actinophylla*

*Schinus molle* var. *areira*

flattened silky hairs on the undersides. The white willow makes a good windbreak tree, but has invasive roots. '**Britzensis**' (syn. 'Chermesina') has bright red stems; '**Chrysostela**' has yellow shoots tipped with orange; *Salix alba* var. *caerulea* has blue-green leaves and is the willow from which cricket bats are made; *S. a.* var. *sericea* has silvery foliage; and '**Vitellina**', the golden willow, has young growth of a brilliant clear yellow. Zones 2–10.

### Salix babylonica

**Weeping willow, Babylon weeping willow**

Probably the most widely grown and easily recognized willow, this Chinese species grows to about 50 ft (15 m) high and wide. Narrow, bright green leaves, 3–6 in (8–15 cm) long, densely cover the flexible, arching branches, which often droop right down to ground level. The catkins are insignificant. '**Crispa**' has twisted leaves and a narrower growth habit. *Salix babylonica* var. *pekinensis* '**Tortuosa**' has bright green lance-shaped, serrated leaves that turn yellow in autumn. *Salix matsudana* is hardly distinguishable from *S. babylonica* but is smaller-growing. Zones 4–10.

## SCHEFFLERA

**syns** *Brassaia, Dizygotheca, Heptapleurum*

This vast genus of small trees, shrubs and scrambling climbers includes over 700 species from most of the wetter tropical and subtropical regions of the world. Leaves consist of similar-sized leaflets arranged like a cartwheel at the ends of long stalks. Small flowers are in branching, usually radiating spikes. Fruit is small, fleshy berries. In their native rainforests many schefflera grow as epiphytes on other trees or rocks. Several are popular house plants in cool and cold climates; a few species are grown for their luxuriant foliage.

### Cultivation

In warm to hot climates plant in a spot sheltered from wind in the sun or part-shade. Young plants make excellent tub specimens. Grow in well-drained, preferably enriched soil; keep moist over summer. Propagate from fresh seed in late summer, cuttings in summer or by air-layering in spring.

### Schefflera actinophylla

syn. *Brassaia actinophylla*
**Queensland umbrella tree, Australian ivy palm, Octopus tree**

Each leaf of this plant resembles an umbrella and consists of 7 to 15 light green, glossy leaflets up to 15 in (38 cm) long. From rainforests of northern Australia and New Guinea, this species grows to 40 ft (12 m) in cultivation, with multiple erect trunks and a dense canopy 20 ft (6 m) wide. Numerous clusters of flowers are arranged in spectacular radiating spikes on red stems; these appear near the top of the plant from late summer to early spring. Each ruby-red flower has contrasting cream stamens and is rich in nectar. Reddish fleshy berries follow. Zones 10–12.

## SCHINUS

The 30 species of evergreen shrubs and trees from this genus, indigenous to Central and South America, are grown for their graceful habit and resistance to very dry conditions. Leaves usually consist of many leaflets but are sometimes simple. The flowers are tiny and arranged in clusters, male and female flowers on the same or separate trees. Female trees feature attractive round berries. They make excellent shade and street trees.

### Cultivation

Plant these marginally frost-hardy to frost-tender plants in a site in full sun in well-drained, coarse soil; they grow best in warm to hot climates. Propagate from fresh seed in spring or cuttings in summer.

*stiff, upward-facing needles, like the ribs of an umbrella, give the Japanese umbrella tree its name.*

*Sciadopitys verticillata*

*Sophora japonica*

### Schinus molle var. areira

**syn. Schinus areira**

**Pepper tree, Peppercorn**

This fast-growing tree with graceful, drooping leaves and branchlets develops an attractive, gnarled trunk as it ages to 30–50 ft (9–15 m) tall. The dark green, shiny leaves are 6 in (15 cm) long, composed of 10 to 18 pairs of small pointed leaflets; they are resinous and aromatic when crushed. Pendulous clusters of tiny cream flowers appear from late spring to early summer. Decorative sprays of tiny rose pink berries follow; these have a peppery taste and have been used like pepper, but are somewhat toxic. In hot dry climates it naturalizes readily and may become a weed. Zones 9–11.

## SCIADOPITYS

*Japanese umbrella pine*

This genus consists of just one species, a very distinctive and handsome conifer from Japan. It is very slow-growing, eventually forming an upright, single-trunked, conical tree to over 100 ft (30 m) tall. It can be kept in a container for long periods and is often used as a bonsai subject.

## Cultivation

*Sciadopitys* prefers a cool maritime climate with cool, moist, humus-rich soil and light shade when young. Propagate from seed.

### Sciadopitys verticillata

The distinctive foliage of this species is composed of deep green, flattened needles, up to 6 in (15 cm) long, carried in stiff whorls of 20 to 30 and facing upward, like the ribs of an umbrella. Interestingly, the needles are not true leaves at all but they do photosynthesize; the true 'leaves' are the tiny scales that lie almost flat along the stems. The small oval cones take 2 years to mature. Zones 5–10.

## SOPHORA

This legume genus of some 50 species of deciduous and evergreen trees, shrubs and perennials is scattered widely through warmer parts of the world. All have pinnate leaves and short racemes of clusters of pea-flowers, mostly in shades of yellow, cream, grayish-blue or lilac. The seed pods are constricted between the seeds and are often slow to split open; the very hard, waxy seeds are long-lived and resistant to water penetration. An interesting group of closely related species, which some botanists believe should be treated as a separate genus, *Edwardsia*, are widely scattered around the southern oceans on small islands such as Easter Island, Gough Island and Mauritius as well as larger landmasses such as New Zealand, Hawaii, and the southern tip of South America; typified by the New Zealand *Sophora tetraptera*, they have large yellow flowers and pods with 4 slightly translucent wings. Their seeds are resistant to saltwater, and are believed to have floated around the southern oceans, with limited evolution taking place after establishing in new lands.

## Cultivation

Sophoras thrive under a wide range of conditions. They can be grown in small groves, or used as shade trees or lawn specimens. Most prefer moist, well-drained soil in sun or part-shade. Propagate from seed or cuttings.

### Sophora japonica

**Japanese pagoda tree, Pagoda tree**

Despite its name, this deciduous tree originates from central China and Korea. It grows to about 100 ft (30 m) high. The light green pinnate leaves are 8 in (20 cm) long, and the cream or occasionally pale pink flowers are borne in long panicles. The pods that follow are like bead necklaces. '**Pendula**' is often grafted onto 8 ft (2.4 m) standards to produce a small weeping tree. Zones 4–10.

*Sophora tetraptera*

*Sorbus aucuparia*

*Pale to golden yellow pea-flowers in spring, borne in showy pendulous clusters, are the hallmark of Kowhai.*

### Sophora tetraptera

**Kowhai**

This free-flowering, usually evergreen tree from the North Island is New Zealand's national flower. It may grow to 30 ft (9 m) tall but usually less. Mature specimens develop a semi-pendulous habit, with interlocking branches. Leaves consist of 20 to 30 pairs of small, gray-green leaflets. The abundant spring pea-flowers are about 1½ in (35 mm) long; pale to golden yellow, they are borne in showy pendulous clusters. Fruit are narrow pods that ripen to dark gray. Zones 8–10.

## SORBUS

Rowan, Service tree, Mountain ash

This genus is made up of 100 species of deciduous trees and shrubs from cool climates of the northern hemisphere, grown for their foliage, timber and decorative fruits. Most species have pinnate leaves and terminal clusters of small, creamy-white flowers in spring. The flowers, often rather unpleasantly scented, are followed by showy berries. A few species have attractive autumn foliage.

#### Cultivation

Rowans are easily grown in sun or part-shade in any well-drained, fertile soil and are most at home in areas with distinct winters. The species may be raised from stratified seed; selected forms are usually grafted. They are susceptible to fireblight.

### Sorbus aria

**Whitebeam**

This European species grows to 30 ft (9 m) tall. Its coarsely toothed, simple leaves, 4 in (10 cm) long, have white felting on the undersides and develop orange and yellow autumn tones. The ½ in (12 mm) berries are red. This species is very tough, tolerating chalky soil, salt winds and air pollution. '**Aurea**' has light yellowish green leaves; '**Chrysophylla**' has yellow leaves; '**Lutescens**' has young foliage covered with fine silvery hairs; '**Majestica**' has leaves and berries larger than those of the species; and '**Theophrasta**' has orange berries and glossy green foliage. Zones 2–9.

### Sorbus aucuparia

**Rowan, Mountain ash, European mountain ash**

The most commonly grown species, this tree grows to about 50 ft (15 m) high in gardens, much taller in its native European and Asian forests. The 11 to 15 small, toothed leaflets turn rich gold in autumn. The white spring flowers are followed by scarlet berries. '**Asplenifolia**' has very finely cut leaves; '**Edulis**' is a large-berried form used for jams and preserves; '**Fructu Luteo**' has orange-yellow berries; '**Pendula**' has wide-spreading growth and a weeping habit; '**Sheerwater Seedling**' is narrowly upright; and '**Xanthocarpa**' has yellow berries. Zones 2–9.

### Sorbus cashmiriana

**Kashmir mountain ash**

Indigenous to the western Himalayas, this spreading tree can attain a height of 25 ft (8 m), although it is often smaller. Its mid-green leaves are made up of 17 to 19 elliptical leaflets, which are gray-green underneath. The pendent clusters of white to pale pink flowers appear in early summer, followed by ½ in (12 mm) wide globular white fruit that endures into winter. Zones 5–9.

## STEWARTIA

syn. *Stuartia*

This eastern Asian and North American genus consists of 15 to 20 species of deciduous or evergreen small trees or shrubs closely allied to the camellias. The flowers are usually white with prominent golden stamens, about 3 in (8 cm)

*Stewartia pseudocamellia*  *Styrax obassia*  *Syzygium paniculatum*

across, and resemble single camellia blooms. The leaves are elliptical, 2–6 in (5–15 cm) long, and often develop bright orange and red autumn tones.

## Cultivation
Best grown in moist, humus-rich, well-drained, slightly acid soil in sun or part-shade. Propagate from seed in autumn or cuttings in summer.

### Stewartia pseudocamellia

syn. *Stuartia pseudocamellia*
**False camellia, Japanese stewartia**

Indigenous to Japan (not Hokkaido) and Korea, this species can grow to 70 ft (21 m) high in the wild, but is more commonly about 20 ft (6 m) in cultivation. It blooms from late spring to early summer and the white flowers are followed by small, spherical, nut-like seed capsules, which are a prominent feature from mid-summer. It has attractive peeling bark and yellow, orange and red autumn foliage. **Stewartia pseudocamellia var. koreana** (syn. *S. koreana*) hardly differs from the typical Japanese species; its distinguishing features are flowers with spreading, not cupped, petals and leaves that are broader and less silky when young. Zones 6–10.

## STYRAX
*Snowbell*

This genus consists of about 100 species of deciduous and evergreen shrubs and small trees occurring naturally over a wide area of the Americas and eastern Asia, with one species native to Europe. Several cool-temperate, deciduous species are cultivated for their neat growth habit and attractive spring display of slightly drooping sprays of small, bell-shaped, white flowers, which appear on the previous year's wood.

## Cultivation
They prefer cool, moist, well-drained soil and cool, moist, summer climates. Usually raised from stratified seed in autumn, they can also be grown from cuttings in summer.

### Styrax obassia

**Fragrant snowbell**

Indigenous to Japan, Korea and northern China, this species grows to 30 ft (9 m) high. Its flowers, less pendulous than those of other species, are slightly fragrant. Large deep green, paddle-shaped leaves, up to 8 in (20 cm) long, have whitish down underneath. It is worth growing for the foliage alone. Zones 6–9.

## SYZYGIUM
*Lillypilly, Brush cherry*

These 400 to 500 species of evergreen trees and shrubs, once part of the genus *Eugenia*, are from tropical and subtropical rainforests of Southeast Asia, Australia and Africa. They have attractive foliage, flowers and berries. The white, pink, magenta or purple edible berries ripen in late summer to autumn. The plants have a dense canopy of shiny green leaves with contrasting red, pink or copper spring growth. Spring and summer flowers are mostly small with protruding white to mauve or crimson stamens giving a fluffy appearance.

## Cultivation
The plants prefer full sun to part-shade and deep, moist, well-drained, humus-rich soil; they do best in warm climates with only occasional light frosts. Prune to shape if necessary. Propagate from fresh seed in spring or cuttings in summer.

### Syzygium paniculatum

syn. *Eugenia paniculata*
**Magenta brush cherry, Australian brush cherry**

This small to medium Australian tree grows to 50–60 ft (15–18 m) with an irregular rounded and

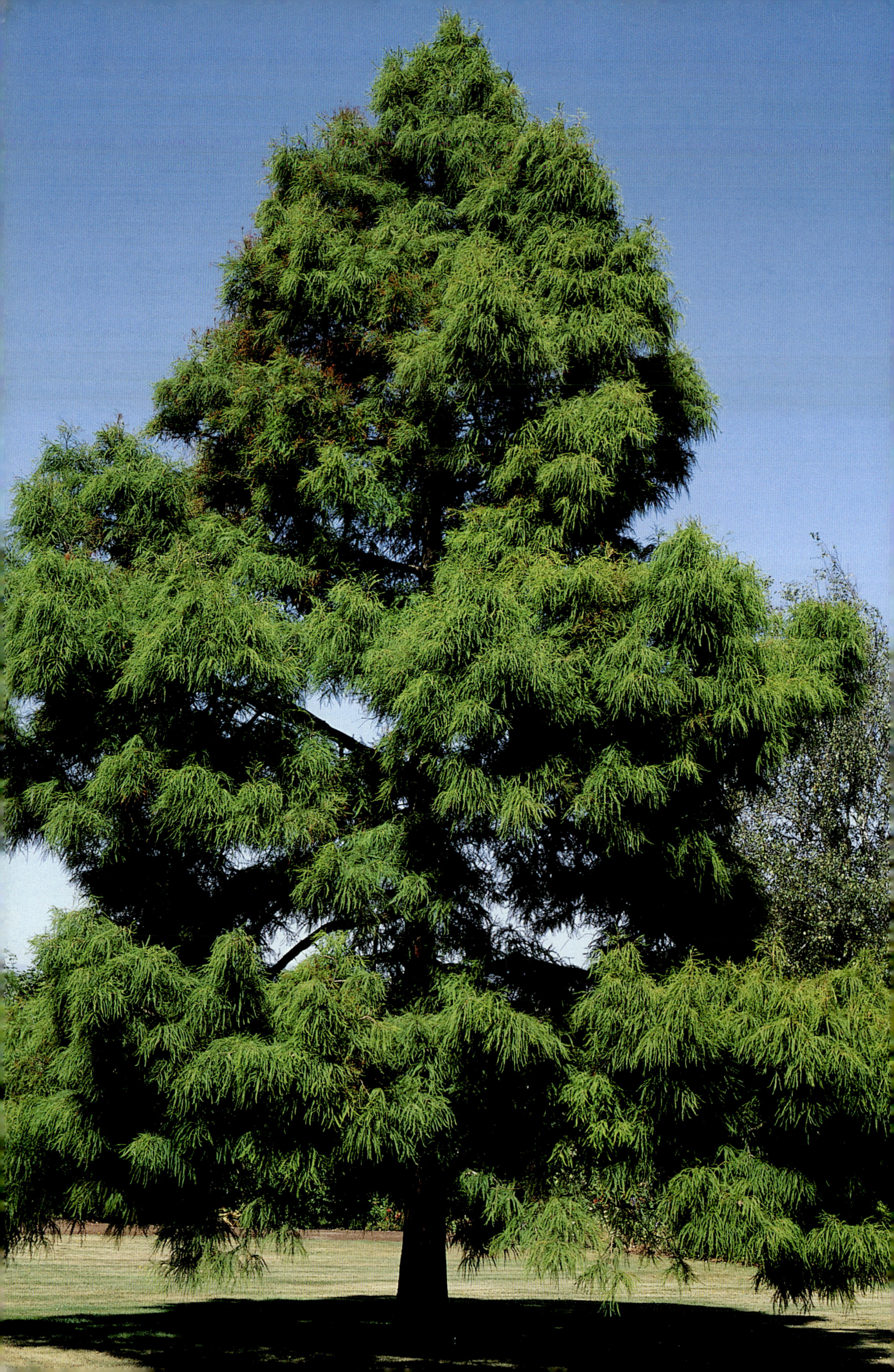

*Taxus baccata*  *Taxodium distichum*

densely foliaged crown. Leaves are shiny green, variable in shape from oval to rounded, coppery brown when young and held on reddish stalks. Fragrant creamy white flowers are ½ in (12 mm) wide and borne in dense clusters, mainly in late spring. The large, decorative fruit is rose purple, oval to rounded and up to 1 in (25 mm) long. This species is used as a hedge in southeastern and southwestern USA. Zones 9–12.

## TAXODIUM

This small genus of deciduous or semi-evergreen conifers consists of 3 species, which occur naturally on the edges of rivers and lakes in eastern North America and parts of Mexico. The genus name comes from the supposed similarity of their foliage to that of the yews (*Taxus*). *Taxodium* species develop large, spreading branches and shed their leaves in autumn, still attached to the small branchlets. These are feather-like and turn coppery brown. The male (pollen) cones are tiny; the female ones are globular, up to 1 in (25 mm) in diameter. The wood of *Taxodium* species is strong, tough and termite resistant.

## Cultivation

These trees thrive in boggy soils in full sun and will even grow in shallow water. However, they will grow equally well in a normal well-drained soil that is sufficiently deep and moist. Propagate from seed or cuttings.

### *Taxodium distichum*

**Bald cypress, Swamp cypress**

Found in the swamp regions of southeastern USA, this fast-growing tree reaches a height of 120 ft (36 m) in the wild, but only about 80 ft (24 m) in cultivation. It is distinguished by its deeply fissured, fibrous, reddish-brown bark and knobbly 'knees'. These special structures are vertical woody growths sent up from the roots when the plant is standing in water and are thought to allow the tree to breathe with its root system submerged. It has tiny, light green, slender, pointed leaves which, as they mature, turn rusty red in autumn then golden brown before falling. It has resinous, round, purple cones, 1 in (25 mm) across. Zones 6–10.

## TAXUS

Yew

The evergreen conifers of this small genus, from cool-climate regions of the northern hemisphere, are slow growing but very long-lived. Young trees are conical in shape, but as they age—over the centuries—they develop a domed crown and a massive, thick trunk clothed in reddish-brown or grayish-brown bark that peels off in thin scales. The flat green leaves are shortish, needle-like and sharply pointed; male and female flowers are borne on separate trees in spring. The single, small brown seed of the female plant is enclosed in a vivid red, fleshy cup; this cup is the only part of the plant that is not poisonous to humans and animals. Yews make excellent dense hedges and are often used for topiary.

## Cultivation

These frost-hardy trees tolerate a wide range of conditions, including heavy shade and chalky soil. However, they do not enjoy warm winters or hot, dry summers. Propagate from seed or cuttings or by grafting.

### *Taxus baccata*

**English yew, Common yew**

Indigenous to western Asia, North Africa and Europe, this dense, dark tree has had legendary and religious associations for centuries. The wood of this tree was once used for making longbows. It grows best in a moist alkaline soil in an open

Opposite: *Taxodium distichum*

*Thuja occidentalis* 'Smaragd'

*Thuja plicata* 'Zebrina'

position. The dark-colored trunk is erect and very thick in maturity; the leaves are dark green. The male tree bears scaly cones, while the female tree bears cup-shaped, scarlet berries which encase a poisonous seed. Old trees may reach 50 ft (15 m), but cultivars rarely achieve this height. '**Aurea**' has golden yellow foliage when young, turning green in the second year. '**Dovastoniana**', known as the Westfelton yew because the original tree was planted in 1777 at Westfelton in Shropshire, England, is a distinct form with tiers of wide-spreading, horizontal branches; it normally is found only in the female form. '**Dovastoniana Aurea**' is similar in habit but the leaves are edged bright yellow. '**Fastigiata**', the Irish yew, is columnar, while '**Repandens**' has a spreading habit. '**Semperaurea**' is a slow-growing male bush with ascending branches and gold leaves that fade with age to a russet yellow. Zones 5–10.

## THUJA
*Arbor-vitae*

This small genus contains 5 evergreen conifers from high-rainfall, cool-temperate regions of northeastern Asia and North America. All are valuable timber trees and several are widely cultivated on a commercial basis. They feature erect, straight trunks covered in deeply fissured, fibrous bark and are columnar to pyramidal in habit. The aromatic foliage consists of sprays of scale-like leaves, often flattened. The egg-shaped cones are covered with overlapping scales and are green, maturing to brown; they are notably small for such large trees, mostly less than ½ in (12 mm) long. Dwarf cultivars, some no more than 15 in (38 cm) high, make excellent rockery or container specimens; most are juvenile forms.

## Cultivation
These plants tolerate cold and are not fussy about soil as long as it is well-drained; most species prefer full sun and dislike dry conditions. Propagation is from seed or cuttings in winter.

### *Thuja occidentalis*

**American arbor-vitae, White cedar**

Growing to 50 ft (15 m) in height with a pyramidal crown, this species has attractive, reddish-brown, peeling bark. Its dense foliage is composed of yellow-green glandular leaves with bluish undersides held on flat, spreading branchlets. The leaves turn bronze in autumn, and tiny, yellow-green cones are produced, which ripen to brown. This species has given rise to more than 140 cultivars, which range from dwarf shrubs to large trees. Zones 4–10.

### *Thuja plicata*

**Western red cedar**

This fast-growing conifer reaches about 80 ft (24 m) in cultivation, but is much taller in its natural habitat. It has long been harvested for its durable and versatile softwood timber. Of conical habit, it becomes columnar in maturity, with branches sweeping the ground. When the rich, coppery-green foliage is crushed, it exudes a sweet, tangy aroma. '**Zebrina**', growing to 20 ft (6 m) high and 5 ft (1.5 m) wide, has glossy bright green foliage striped with yellow. Zones 5–10.

## TILIA
*Lime tree, Linden*

From temperate regions of Asia, Europe and North America, this genus consists of 45 species of tall, handsome, deciduous trees, often planted in avenues and streets because they are fast-growing and withstand regular heavy pruning and atmospheric pollution. They are generally upright, with thick, buttressed trunks, and have a tendency to sucker. Rounded to heart-shaped leaves, held on thin stalks, briefly turn yellow in autumn. The

*Caption*

*Tilia cordata*   *Ulmus americana*

small, fragrant, cup-shaped cream flowers are borne in clusters in summer; each cluster has a whitish bract, which persists and helps to disperse the fruit on the wind. Both flowers and bracts are dried to make linden tea. The fruits are small, round, hard, green berries. Several species are valued for their pale, strong but lightweight wood.

## Cultivation

Very frost hardy, they do best in cool climates and prefer full sun, neutral, well-drained soil and plenty of water in dry periods. Even quite large trees can be readily transplanted during their winter dormancy. Propagate from seed in autumn, from cuttings or by layering; selected forms and hybrids can be grafted in late summer.

### Tilia cordata

**syn. *Tilia parvifolia***
**Small-leafed linden, Little-leaf linden**

An inhabitant of European woodlands, this species grows to 100 ft (30 m) tall with a dome-shaped crown. Its leathery leaves, 2 in (5 cm) across, are bright green on top with pale undersides. Its small flowers are pale yellow and sweetly scented; the fruit is gray. This long-lived species can make a handsome specimen for parks and formal gardens where it has plenty of space. The soft whitish timber is often used for wood carving and musical instruments. '**Greenspire**' is a fast-growing American selection with an upright habit and oval-shaped crown. '**June Bride**' is heavy-flowering with conical growth and glossy leaves. Zones 2–9.

### Tilia × europaea

**syn. *Tilia × vulgaris***
**European linden, Common lime tree**

Widely grown in Europe, this handsome, vigorous hybrid between *Tilia cordata* and *T. platyphyllos* grows to 100 ft (30 m) tall. It is characterized by a dense, shapely crown held on a stout trunk, which has a strong tendency to sucker. Shoots should be removed from the burl at the base from time to time. The smooth green shoots grow in a distinct zigzag pattern and the bright green, rounded to heart-shaped leaves have toothed edges. Its pale yellow flowers appear among the leaves in early summer; they are sometimes infused and drunk as a tea. The rounded fruit are faintly ribbed. The foliage of '**Wratislaviensis**' is golden yellow when young, maturing to a dark green. Zones 3–9.

## Ulmus
Elm

The 30 or so species in this genus of trees occur naturally in temperate regions of the northern hemisphere. In Europe and North America elm trees have been devastated by Dutch elm disease, caused by the fungus *Ophiostoma ulmi*, which is transmitted by the elm bark beetle. All but a few east-Asian species are deciduous, turning yellow in autumn. The leaves, usually one-sided at the base, have prominent, parallel lateral veins and regularly toothed margins; the small, disc-like fruits have a membranous wing and are carried in clusters. Most elms are large-limbed with furrowed gray bark and high, domed crowns.

## Cultivation

Mostly very frost hardy, they require cool to cold winters and prefer full sun and deep, moist, fertile soil. Propagate from semi-ripe cuttings in summer, from suckers or by grafting or budding in autumn. Propagation from seed in autumn yields low germination rates.

### Ulmus americana

**American elm, White elm**

The largest North American elm, this species occurs naturally over eastern and central USA, and

*Ulmus glabra*

*Zelkova serrata*

*Zelkova's sharply serrated leaves turn golden yellow to rusty brown in autumn.*

southern Canada. It can reach a height of 120 ft (36 m) in the wild—about half that in cultivation—and has high-arching limbs. Mature trees develop a broad crown and may become strongly buttressed at the base; the ash-gray bark is deeply fissured. The leaves, 4–6 in (10–15 cm) long, have smooth upper-sides with slightly downy undersides, and unforked lateral veins. '**Delaware**' is broadly vase-shaped, fast-growing and claimed to be resistant to Dutch elm disease. '**Princeton**' is also vase-shaped, and vigorous with some resistance to elm leaf beetle. '**Washington**' is thought to be a hybrid of *Ulmus americana* and an unknown species. Zones 3–9.

### Ulmus glabra

**syns *Ulmus montana*, *U. scabra***
**Scotch elm, Wych elm**

This major European elm can grow to more than 100 ft (30 m) high with a wide, spreading crown, and does not sucker from the roots. Its dull, dark green leaves, up to 6 in (15 cm) long and broadest near the apex, have a rough raspy upper surface. '**Camperdownii**' forms a dome-like mound of weeping branches when grafted onto a standard; '**Lutescens**', the common golden elm, has spring and summer foliage colored lime green and tipped with pale yellow. Zones 3–9.

### Ulmus procera

**English elm**

This elm, which can reach 150 ft (45 m) in height, has a high-branched, billowing crown and straight or slightly sinuous trunk. In the UK, few have survived Dutch elm disease. Cultivated in the southern hemisphere, it produces a compact, rounded crown up to 80 ft (24 m) high. Its smallish, rounded leaves have a rough surface. Seldom setting fertile seed, it is usually propagated from suckers. The rare cultivar '**Louis van Houtte**' has golden-green leaves. Zones 4–9.

## ZELKOVA

Occurring naturally from Asia Minor across cool-climate areas of western Asia to China and Japan, these deciduous trees are cultivated for their attractive habit and handsome foliage. They are important timber trees in China and Japan. The leaves resemble those of the English or American elms, but are smaller, giving an effect of airy elegance. Although related to the elms, they are not plagued by the same diseases and are becoming popular as elm substitutes. The small, greenish flowers, borne in spring, may be perfumed; both these and the fruits are insignificant.

### Cultivation

Although frost hardy, they prefer some shelter. They need full sun and deep, fertile, well-drained soil and plenty of water during summer. Propagate from seed or root cuttings in autumn, or by grafting.

### Zelkova serrata

**Japanese zelkova**

This ornamental tree from Japan, Korea and Taiwan grows to a height of 80 ft (24 m) or more with a wide, spreading crown. It has smooth bark, dappled gray and brown, and new shoots are tinged purple. The pointed, oblong, sharply serrated leaves are dull green and slightly hairy above, with shiny undersides. The foliage turns golden yellow to rusty brown in autumn. Cultivars include '**Village Green**', and '**Green Vase**', growing to 40 ft (12 m) tall in a graceful vase shape. Zones 3–10.

# Index of common names & synonyms

In this book, genus names are already listed in alphabetical order. For this reason the index contains only common names and synonyms that have different genus names.

## A

Amur cork tree, 68
apples, 59
apricot, Japanese, 76
arbor-vitae, 92
ashes, 48
aspens, 74–5
Atlas cedar, 34
Australian brush cherry, 89, 91
Australian daphne, 71
Australian frangipani, 51
Australian ivy palm, 86
Australian pine, 33

## B

Babylon weeping willow, 86
bald cypress, 91
bay tree, 57
bead tree, 62
beeches, 47–8
    southern, 64
*Benthamia fragifera*, 39
birches, 31–2
box elder, 24
bracelet honey myrtle, 60
*Brassaia*, 86
brush cherry, 89, 91
buckeye, 26
Buddhist pine, 74
bull bay, 59

## C

cabbage trees, 38
camphor laurel, 36
Canary Islands pine, 69
canoe birch, 32
Carriere hawthorn, 41
catalpa, 33–4
cedars, 34–5
    Japanese, 41
chennar, 72
cherries, 75
    flowering, 76–9
cherry plum, 76
chinaberry, 62
chinar, 72
claret ash, 48
coast banksia, 31
cock's comb, 45
Colorado fir, 22
Colorado spruce, 68–9
coral trees, 45
cork oak, 82

cornelian cherry, 39
cornels, 38–9
cottonwoods, 74–5
crabapples, 59–60
crape (or crepe) myrtle, 56
cypresses, 43–4
    false, 35–6

## D

*Dendrobenthamia capitata*, 39
*Dizgotheca*, 86
dogwoods, 38–9
Douglas fir, 79–80
dove tree, 44
*Dracaena australis*, 38

## E

Eastern red cedar, 55
elms, 93–4
empress tree, 67
English elm, 94
English hawthorn, 40–1
English holly, 52
English oak, 82
English walnut, 53
English yew, 91–2
epaulette tree, 80
*Eucalyptus ficifolia*, 40
European ash, 48
European aspen, 75
European beech, 47–8
European hornbeam, 33
European larch, 57
European linden, 93
European mountain ash, 88

## F

false acacia, 84
false camellia, 89
false cypress, 35
Father David's maple, 24
firs, 22
frangipani, 72
    Australian, 51
funereal cypress, 43–4

## G

gean, 75
golden chain tree, 55–6
golden mimosa, 23
golden rain tree, 55
golden wattle, 23
gum trees, 45–6

## H

handkerchief tree, 44
hawthorns, 40–1
*Heptapleurum*, 86
higan cherry, 77
Highclere holly, 52
Himalayan birch, 32
Himalayan strawberry tree, 39
hollies, 52
holly / holm oak, 81–2
honey locust, 50
hornbeam, 32–3
horoeka, 79
horse-chestnuts, 26–7

## I

Indian bean tree, 33–4
Italian cypress, 43–4

## J

Japanese apricot, 76
Japanese black pine, 70
Japanese cedar, 41
Japanese crab, 60
Japanese maple, 24, 26
Japanese pagoda tree, 87
Japanese red pine, 69–70
Japanese stewartia, 89
Japanese umbrella pine, 87
Japanese zelkova, 94
Judas tree, 35
juneberry, 28
junipers, 53–5

## K

kaffirboom, 45
karo, 71
Kashmir cypress, 43
kowhai, 88
kusamaki, 74

## L

lancewood, 79
larches, 56–7
laurels, 57
Lavalle hawthorn, 41
Lawson cypress, 36
lemonwood, 71
Leyland cypress, 43
ligiri, 51–2
lillypilly, 89

95 TREES

lily-of-the-valley tree, 38
lime trees, 92–3
lindens, 92–3
locust, 50
    black, 83–4
Lombardy poplar, 75
London plane, 72
loquat, 44–5
love tree, 35

## M
madrone, 29
magenta brush cherry, 89, 91
mahogany pine, 74
maidenhair tree, 48–50
maples, 23–6
may, 40–1
mazzard, 75
Mediterranean cypress, 43–4
Mexican weeping pine, 70
midland hawthorn, 40–1
monkey puzzle, 28–9
Monterey cypress, 43
mountain ash, 88
mulberries, 63–4
myrobalan, 76
myrtle beech, 64

## N
narrow-leafed black
    peppermint, 46
narrow-leaved ash, 48
*Neopanax*, 79
New Zealand cabbage tree, 38
New Zealand Christmas tree, 63
New Zealand lacebark, 51
New Zealand silver beech, 64
Norfolk Island pine, 29
*Nothopanax*, 79

## O
oaks, 81–2
octopus tree, 86
old man banksia, 31
olives, 65
Oregon pine, 79–80
osiers, 84–6

## P
pagoda tree, 87
paper birch, 32
paperbark maple, 24
paperbarks, 60–2
pears, 80–1
pencil cedar, 55
pepper tree, 87
pepperidge, 65
Persian lilac, 62

Persian walnut, 53
Persian witch-hazel, 67
pin oak, 82
pines, 69–70
planes, 71–2
plum pine, 72, 74
plums, 76
pohutukawa, 63
poplars, 74–5
Port Orford cedar, 36
pride of India, 56
princess tree, 67
punk tree, 60, 62

## Q
Queensland umbrella tree, 86

## R
redbud, 35
red-flowering gum, 40
redwood, dawn, 62
Rocky Mountain fir, 22
Roman pine, 70
rosary tree, 62
rose acacia, 84
rosebud cherry, 77
rowan, 88

## S
sallows, 84–6
Sargent cherry, 76
saucer magnolia, 59
saw banksia, 31
Sawara cypress, 36
Scotch elm, 94
Scots pine, 70
Serbian spruce, 68
service tree, 88
serviceberry, 28
she-oaks, 33
silk tree, 28
silkworm mulberries, 64
silver birch, 32
silver pear, 81
siris, 27
snow gum, 46
snowbell, 89
snowy mespilus, 28
sorrel tree, 65–7
sour gum, 65
sourwood, 65–7
South African coral tree, 45
South Australian blue gum, 46
southern beeches, 64
southern catalpa, 34
southern magnolia, 59
southern rata, 63
Spanish fir, 22
spruces, 68–9

strawberry tree, 29
subalpine fir, 22
sugi, 41
swamp cypress, 91
sweet bay, 57
sweet cherry, 75
sweet gum, 58
sweet pittosporum, 71
sweetshade, 51
Sycamore maple, 26
sycamores, 71–2
Sydney golden wattle, 23

## T
table dogwood, 39
Taiwan cherry, 75
tarata, 71
Tasmanian beech, 64
temple tree, 72
ti kouka, 38
Tibetan cherry, 77
Tokyo cherry, 77, 79
totara, 74
tree of heaven, 27
tulip tree, 58
tupelo, 64–5

## U
ulmo, 47
umbrella pine, 70

## V
varnish tree, 55
Voss laburnum, 56

## W
walnuts, 53
Waterer laburnum, 56
wattles, 22–3
weeping silver pear, 81
western red cedar, 92
white cedar, 62, 92
white ironbark, 46
whitebeam, 88
wild cherry, 75
willow leaf peppermint, 46
willow-leafed pear, 81
willows, 84–6
wing nut, 80
wonder tree, 51–2
wych elm, 94

## Y
yew pine, 74
yews, 91–2
Yoshino cherry, 77, 79